DOWN AND OUT
IN PATAGONIA, KAMCHATKA AND TIMBUKTU

First published in 2014 by Motorbooks, a member of Quayside Publishing Group, 400 First Avenue North, Suite 400, Minneapolis, MN 55401 USA

Motorbooks titles are also available at discounts in bulk quantity for industrial or sales-promotional use. For details write to Special Sales Manager at Quayside Publishing Group, 400 First Avenue North, Suite 400, Minneapolis, MN 55401 USA.

To find out more about our books, visit us online at www.motorbooks.com.

ISBN-13: 978-0-7603-4583-2

Library of Congress Cataloging-in-Publication Data

Printed in China

10 9 8 7 6 5 4 3 2 1

Editor: Jordan Wiklund
Design Manager: Brad Springer
Cover Designer: Simon Larkin
Layout Designer: Diana Boger

On the front cover: Dr. Frazier's crashed motorcycle in the American desert.

On the back cover: Resting with the camels in the African desert (top); matching the lean of the Leaning Tower of Pisa (center); Chinese yaks aren't quite as fast as motorcycles (bottom).

On the front flap: Down and out in Taiwan, and exploring the Golden Triangle in northern Thailand.

On the back flap: Stuck in the Sahara sand.

DOWN AND OUT

IN PATAGONIA, KAMCHATKA AND TIMBUKTU

Greg Frazier's Round and Round and Round the World Motorcycle Journey

DR. GREGORY W. FRAZIER

motorbooks

CONTENTS

A MOTORCYCLE LIFE

Motorcycle Cool

"No motorcycle for you!" My 5-foot-1-inch Quaker mother was adamant about my not buying a motorcycle, and she was backed up by my Marine Corps father, who believed sparing the rod would spoil the child.

What a long, wild ride it's been to get here—more than a million miles and 50 years.

I had grown up rolling across ground on a variety of nonmotorized vehicles: at age one, I was on a four-wheel cart, a push car. By two years old, I had graduated to a tricycle.

My family came from a Quaker background. My parents met at a Quaker college, and I was born into that religion as a third-generation Quaker. I was brought up under many of the religion's teachings, such as how to be frugal and the importance of saving money.

In my early teens, I wanted the usual toys many children desire, but I especially wanted a bicycle. To graduate to two wheels, though, my parents wanted me to purchase it from either the small allowance they gave me or from earning money from work. I was barely a teenager. Finding work was nearly impossible, and the suburb where we lived outside Portland, Oregon, was starved for jobs.

My off-road adventures began in 1948 by my not knowing my personal riding envelope or the limits of the vehicle I was driving.

My thirst for a bicycle, though, could not be squelched by merely lacking enough monthly allowance. I came up with a plan and pitched it to my parents. If they lent me the money to purchase a bicycle, I would pay them back from what I earned by delivering newspapers, for which I needed, of course, the bicycle. For me, it made sense.

A deal was struck, and I became a newspaper delivery boy, riding my three-speed Raleigh bicycle through the neighborhood after school on weekdays and early on Sunday mornings. It took me less than a year to pay back my parents.

The side benefit to having a bicycle was I could explore neighborhoods far from my home base when not in school or tossing newspapers. The bicycle was my ticket to freedom from a strict disciplinarian father and his militaristic household.

My grandfather had been a physician, working for the government on various Indian reservations. My father was to follow in his footsteps, but after he froze his feet walking out of the Chosin Reservoir Campaign in Korea in 1950, his career in medicine was abandoned for a job as a government bureaucrat, possibly accounting for his stringent household demeanor.

From as early as I can remember, my parents insisted that I had to carry on the family tradition of going to medical school after college and becoming a physician to make up for my father's inability to do the same. Education was a priority in our household, and I strove to achieve good grades so I could be accepted at a college.

I soon had to give up my lucrative paper route. We moved to Billings, Montana, where my father was promoted within the government bureaucracy, but thankfully I was able to keep the bicycle. I was a 14-year-old peddling fool, and I rode my bicycle as often as I could to stay away from the rod my father threatened to use to ensure good grades in school.

I met a girl at school. Her name was Sam, and she was the kind of woman whose body was a magnet to anybody with a pulse. She had sharp features, long black hair, and an hourglass figure. Between my youthfulness, raging male hormones, and the girl's interest in me, my parents were finding my absence from home the reason for lower grades at school, and the bicycle was wrapped up in the center of this. It made me mobile, and mobility brought me to her. Sam was two years older than me, smoked cigarettes, wore a black leather motorcycle jacket, and was the coolest girl in our school. She looked like she had walked out of the movie *The Wild One*. Her disdain for what I saw as the mediocrity of life drew me to her, away from the rod and heavy hand of my father at home.

She liked motorcycles, had been the girlfriend of a motorcyclist at one time, and asked me when I was going to get one so she and I could go riding. I knew nothing about motorcycles other than what I had seen in movies. What I did know was I was going to have to acquire a motorcycle if Sam was to become my girlfriend.

Mike, a boy in one of my classes, owned a moped. It was a 50cc Allstate sold by Sears, Roebuck and Company. Mike and I became friends and he sometimes let me ride on the back of the bike. After several months I managed to talk him into letting me drive the moped, alone. It was a wobbly start, but my bicycling skills managed to keep the moped upright long enough to feel more than a pedaling breeze in the wind. That first solo ride hooked me on motorized two-wheel movement. I also felt I qualified as a motorcycle rider, the kind that my cigarette-smoking and leather-jacket-wearing girlfriend wanted.

My parents were becoming seriously worried. To keep me away from the girl and what my parents saw as a bad influence, I found myself being grounded for the most minor infractions of home rules, such as not cleaning my room on a Monday or losing my winter gloves.

I made up excuses to get away from home, and several times I was caught with Sam or my moped-riding buddy. The rod would whistle through the wind and I would pay a heavy price. One time my father had to stop beating me with his leather belt because his arm had become tired; that was for being seen on the back of my friend's moped when I was supposed to be at school. I did not know if the punishment was for not being at school or for lying about my whereabouts when confronted. The result was the same.

Disaster struck my motorcycling world when my friend ran into an earth mover and crashed. His right leg had to be amputated after the

In 1948, my grandfather gave me the Indian name "Sun Chaser" for trying to catch the sun in the backyard of our house using my four-wheel scooter.

9

By my third birthday, I had advanced from four wheels to three. My parents said they were still unable to keep me on paved surfaces; I was always exploring.

vehicle ran over him and the moped. The accident was well covered by the local news and my parents hammered home how dangerous motorcycles were and how my friend's accident proved their claim. I was forbidden to ride on the back of any motorcycle from that day.

With no motorcycle (much less a friend with a motorcycle), Sam and her black leather jacket slowly drifted away. What she left me with was the belief that anyone with a motorcycle was cool and a taste for cigarettes. Since both my parents smoked, I often snuck one out of their packages and smoked it. After all, it's not like they could smell the after-smoke residue on me.

While I pined for my lost girlfriend, what I missed more was the freedom I had tasted on the seat of Mike's moped. My days and nights were consumed puzzling over how I could get my bike and my girl back.

My parents could see I was looking down a road in life that did not meet with their wants. They belittled my former girlfriend, saying Sam was "trash" and that she was beneath me. To me, she was the coolest girl I had ever met, and if trash was what she was, then trash was what I wanted. As for good grades, medical school, and life as a physician, those goals were no longer high on my list. They had been replaced by getting a motorcycle and getting out of the life I had known.

I finally came up with what I thought was a good plan. I proposed to my parents that they lend me the money I needed to purchase a used motorcycle. I would pay them back by working in the sugar-beet fields as a laborer over the coming summer, something that I had done before. But it wasn't any good. "No! No motorcycle for you," my mother said. "You're going to a private boarding school."

We had discussed attending a private school before. My father had gone to a private Quaker school, and my grandfather had been a student at Dartmouth. What had been sold to me about private school was I would get a better education at a Quaker school than I would locally and therefore would increase my chances at being accepted at a good college or university for my pre-med undergraduate work, which would eventually lead to medical school and finally the fulfillment of the family dream of another "Dr. Frazier."

In 1962, I was shipped off to a Quaker boarding school. At the time, it seemed as far away as imaginable from motorcycles and my biker girl. It wasn't a gift from my parents; it was a curse.

As I sat on the porch of that Quaker School, gazing at another lonely Pennsylvania horizon and having promised my parents I would be a good boy, at age 14, I was down and supposedly out.

Under the Quakers' Thumbs

Within the first month with the Quakers, I was disciplined for smoking cigarettes. I was suspended and sent to live with the school's head master. While being confined, I discovered that I was not safe under

At 14 years old, I was transferred from the hands of my parents to under the thumbs of the authorities at a Quaker private school, where cigarettes and vehicles were banned, and there certainly were no girls wearing black leather motorcycle jackets and skin-tight pants. I promised my parents as they left, "OK, I'll be good."

My parents wanted me to look my best while under the thumbs of the Quakers, so they sent me off as well-dressed as any scrubbed teenager could be in that era. I was not allowed to own a motorcycle.

the thumb of the Quaker headmaster. Despite his repeated attempts to fondle me, I was able to fend him off until my suspension ended and I was able to escape back to regular classes, away from the dirty old man. He was a short man with a bristly mustache that disguised a harelip. When he spoke, his words slithered out from under that mustache, lisping and false.

I was living in what I saw as an unsafe world. Each summer I returned to Montana and told my parents I did not want to go back to that school, and each year they made it clear that I could not live at home or return to the local high school and that I would have to get a job and live on my own. About the only sunlight in my summers was meeting some motorcycle owners who allowed me to hang around while they worked on their cycles, mostly Indians and Harley-Davidsons. They didn't let me ride on the back of their motorcycles or offer one up for one of my own, but they seemed to like my willingness to do anything—from washing parts in gasoline to waxing fenders—just for the privilege of being around them.

The motorcyclists taught me a few things my father did not, such as how to defend myself. I was skinny, weighed less than 120 pounds, and was more than 6 feet tall, gangly and awkward. When I told them about the beatings, they showed me how to hit back, physically and mentally. And the next time my father was about to strike me, I grabbed his left wrist with the belt in it, held it still between us with my right hand, and told him, "If you hit me again, I will hit you back." And that was the last time he hit me. I was 16.

During my last year under the Quaker thumb, I shared a room with Buzz, a friend in the dorm. I was still trying to dodge the headmaster and his unwanted advances. I was afraid to tell Buzz about the dirty old man trying to touch me, thinking I would be viewed as a pretty boy who encouraged the flirtations. The one male teacher I did confide in told me to "forget it, just stay away from him." And that was what I did, until he backed me up against a wall one day. Then the lesson my motorcycle friends taught me kicked in, and I grabbed his hand and told him if he did not stop I would tell other school authorities. That threat and my physical response scared him enough that the advances stopped, and my torment was over.

The highlight of that last year was when my roommate bought a Vespa motor scooter. On weekends we motored away from school and visited his home near West Chester. He drove the scooter and I rode on the back. We embraced the freedom the Vespa offered and rode away from the Quakers.

Neither one of us had a great deal of mechanical knowledge of the workings of a motor scooter. My knowledge of two-wheeled vehicles was from washing motorcycle parts and watching my Montana friends work on their motorcycles. Fortunately for my roommate and me, the Vespa needed little attention, and we were free to roam and ride as long as we added gas and oil.

The one time the Vespa broke down, the shift cable had broken. We were in the middle of Philadelphia and only managed to get home by me pulling on the broken cable by hand whenever he yelled, "Shift!"

Of course, while on these school-approved weekends away, I never told school authorities or my parents I was riding on the back of a motor scooter. Had I done so, I think one or the other would have found a way to limit my freedom. As I'd been told by the male school teacher, I just "stayed away" from the subject, another secret from the authorities.

As I moved toward my last months at the Quaker private school, I became more depressed. College was on the horizon, which I simply equated with more classroom time. Whenever I saw the school headmaster, he leered at me, threatening that any time spent on a motor scooter—the one and best positive aspect of my life—should be limited to a few scant hours riding as passenger. I was down and literally out of motorcycling.

Out from under the Quakers' Thumbs

The Quaker headmaster and I parted ways prior to graduation when I transferred to a special high school in Pittsburgh, Pennsylvania. The Quaker school was no place I wanted to be. At the new school, I made friends with a serious motorhead, but he was more of a car guy than a motorcycle guy. I spent as much time as possible with him whenever I wasn't in school, as he tried to keep his numerous cars running. From him, I learned about basic mechanics, things such as how water was pushed through the cooling system and why a battery was needed for spark. His friends called him Midnight, because that was his preferred time to work in the garage.

He was an interesting guy, but not one I thought my parents needed to meet or know about. He taught me how to buy beer and how to hop a freight train for a free ride between cities, which I did a few times. He also taught me how, while on a freight train carrying car parts, to disconnect a standard transmission from a new car and toss it off the train to be later collected and sold for good cash, although that was a lesson I never applied.

Midnight had a BSA motorcycle. We often worked on it, but it never seemed to want to start, and when it did it would soon quit. He and I labored on that BSA for many weekends, often having to push it back to his house. He would try to kick-start the BSA until he was out of breath and then let me try. About the most satisfaction I got out of his BSA was sitting on it and imagining riding it while he worked on his car. That dream died when he traded it for some car engine. When I asked him if he was going to buy another motorcycle, he told me that he might, but never again an English motorcycle. He said if he bought another motorcycle it would be a Harley-Davidson. It may have been his relationship with his BSA that resulted in my never owning a British-made motorcycle.

The First Motorcycle

Buzz and I kept in touch. He went to college in Pennsylvania while I headed to a small school in Indiana. When he bought a Honda CB 77, I was more than green with envy. I was wildly jealous. I also knew there was no way I could buy a motorcycle on what little money I had while at college. Between my parents and what I could make working in the school kitchen, there was never any money left for anything that did not come with the tuition, room, and board package we were paying.

When my former roommate called me and told me his new college roommate was selling his Honda 305cc Super Hawk, I told him I would buy it. Begging money from a girlfriend and borrowing some money from others, I managed to buy the Honda, and with it, my ticket to freedom.

The Super Hawk let me get away from school and work. I also thought it would somehow help more girls come into my life. The memory of Samantha who had drifted away to a guy who owned a motorcycle haunted me, but the memory faded as I discovered that motorcycles were not girl-catchers, at least not in the way that a net catches fish. They were a means to go fast, to move through the wind and explore places not possible by walking or driving a car. And in those places, I came to learn, I might find some girls anyway.

I did not tell my parents about the new motorcycle. It was not until I arrived home that summer on it that they found out. They had asked how I was going to get home and to my summer job from Indiana, and I answered in vague and uncertain terms. I was afraid they would take it away from me.

When my mother saw that I had arrived home on a motorcycle, she immediately said, "I hope you didn't borrow money to buy that thing." My father refused to speak to me, much less look at what I felt was the single most important thing in my life at that time. The two weeks I spent at their house was like being stranded in the Arctic, where mere exposure to the atmosphere is enough to kill you. Instead of bearing the brunt of the freeze, I left early every morning on the

Honda to spend the day riding as far as I could in the daylight hours. To pay for gas and food I borrowed money from my old motorcycle friends who had let me wash their motorcycle parts or wax fenders, and I promised to pay them back once my summer job started, which I did.

The Honda also started my learning curve in off-pavement riding, which was a dirty riding experience, a nasty and ugly affair, and one not easily forgotten. I still cringe when someone reminds me of my first misstep. Nightmares often replay the event in color. Massive quantities of alcohol have not erased the memory on my cranial hard drive. It was a motorcycle expedition involving too much testosterone, too little common sense, and a little head with no brain doing the thinking, a motorcycle sexpedition.

An invitation from a beautiful 18-year-old woman found this motorcycling greenhorn deciding to take a shortcut to her town over a dirt road instead of wisely going the longer way around on pavement. I had driven over the shortcut before in a car, knowing it could carve at least an hour off the trip between her house and mine. The dirt road was used mostly by local Montana ranchers to move cattle and equipment from one field to another, and though stable enough for cattle and ranch hands, the road was still almost 100 percent dirt.

With the motorcycle gas tank filled and my hormones pumping like a horny monkey amped on methamphetamines, I left the pavement and started across the 20 miles of unpaved track through wheat fields and open prairie. The Honda 305 Super Hawk and I managed fine for the first few miles even though my off-roading learning curve was pointed in a straight line upward.

It took only a few minutes for me to realize the street tires did better in the barren tracks that they did on the grass between the ruts. My learning curve dropped a few more degrees as I learned speed meant loss of control, so I slowed down.

The rain started about a quarter of the way across the fields. It was like many hot afternoon rains in a Montana summer, a black cloud that dumped loads of water in precise areas, often less than a mile wide, as it moved across the fields. The Montana rains leave the air smelling like sagebrush and wheat, a smell not found anywhere else on the planet. The water also turns a dirt-laden ranch road into muck. The mud is not even called mud; it's called gumbo, and it's thick, dark, and difficult. Unlike the Cajun food from which it gets its name, Montana gumbo means nasty gunk that can halt a John Deere tractor in low gear.

When I hit the first bit of gumbo, it caused the handlebars of the Honda to go from left stop to right stop and back to center before I knew what was happening. The front wheel had tried to crawl up one side of a muddy rut and then the other. What saved me from crashing was the narrowness of the rut.

I spent the next 20 to 30 minutes wallowing in first gear from side-to-side in the ruts until they smoothed out and the track became

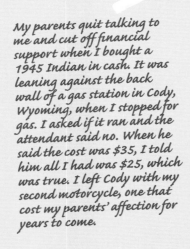

My parents quit talking to me and cut off financial support when I bought a 1945 Indian in cash. It was leaning against the back wall of a gas station in Cody, Wyoming, when I stopped for gas. I asked if it ran and the attendant said no. When he said the cost was $35, I told him all I had was $25, which was true. I left Cody with my second motorcycle, one that cost my parents' affection for years to come.

flat. That section would have taken me only minutes had it been dry, and my testosterone clock was telling my teenage brain if the road returned to ruts for the next 10 to 15 miles, I was going to be very late for my date.

As soon as I was on the flat, I shifted into second gear and then third as the tires seemed to find some grip. I could feel globs of gumbo hit my pants legs but thought that was a good thing, because the tires were throwing off the mud. I also noted I was twisting the throttle more to keep up the speed. When the little red light went off in my big head saying maybe I should stop and look at the wheels, the front wheel locked. I flew over the handlebars and smacked face down with arms outstretched, sliding in the freshly wetted gray Montana gumbo for what seemed like a mile but only amounted to 15 to 20 feet.

I was not hurt, but I looked like a monster from the swamp. Green grass was jammed up the sleeves of my black leather motorcycle

For gas money to drive back east, I agreed to tow a second motorcycle partway. We took the front wheel off that motorcycle and attached the forks to a bumper-mounted trailer hitch. The system worked, except when the Ford would go over a bump, which would bottom-out the rear springs of the Ford and the driveshaft would make a loud grinding noise.

jacket, and gray mud was jammed down the front. I also had mud down the inside of the front of my jeans as well as into the top of my Wellington boots. Nothing on my front was black as all had been before. I looked like a walking nest of sloppy gray muck and some sort of giant wild bird's nest.

The motorcycle had stopped. The clutch lever was broken, and accumulating mud and muck had locked the front wheel. It was wedged solid between the tire and the fender.

My adventure learning curve went down a few more degrees that afternoon as I learned how to remove the front fender with a pair of cheap pliers, shift without using the clutch, and find a chain master link in deep gumbo after the holding clip came off followed by the whole chain itself.

When I finally arrived at my date's house, it was dark. Her parents told me she had waited four or five hours before she went out with her girlfriends. One look at gray-covered Mr. Motorcycle Mud Man standing on their front porch likely had them blessing who or what had whipped me into being late.

When I am asked how I first learned to adventure off-road using a motorcycle, whether it was from being enrolled in a riding school or from racing, I answer with some chagrin mixed with a the dark memory: "It was the result of a motorcycle sexpedition, my first sordid adventure affair."

I sold the Honda that summer. A car had run me off the road in Yellowstone Park and the money needed to make the repairs was more than I had. The buyer cleared up all my debts and I had only my parent's second car for transportation. Without a motorcycle, the rest of the summer felt empty.

My parents were happy that the motorcycle was gone, happy enough even to pay for the upkeep on their car that I was using. Soon I had enough money to buy my own junker, a 1949 Cadillac hearse, after the family Dodge died an ugly death. Even though I had supposedly killed their second car, my father had started to talk to me and my mother became less of a grouch when I spent weekends at their house. All was well in the Frazier family until I bought another motorcycle days before driving back to college.

My parents stopped speaking to me again and withheld some previously promised travel money. If I had enough money to buy a motorcycle, I didn't need their money to pay for gas to get back to college. If I needed food and gas money, I could sell the motorcycle for it.

I left home under a dark family cloud. I was down, but with a travel loan from my Indian motorcycle buddies, I was not out.

CHAPTER TWO

HITTING THE ROAD

The First Motorcycle Trip

Jail. Hookers. Broke. Not bad elements for my first long trip on a motorcycle. At the time, however, it was quite a different story. There was nothing fun about a broken motorcycle, a cold jail cell, and a sleepless night surrounded by a cage filled with fallen doves who made fun of my riding pal, Brian, and me.

My choice for making trips or tours to continue lowering my learning curve was a 74ci Indian Chief.

By spring 1966, I had been using my first motorcycle as a getaway tool from college for days or weekends or even just afterschool evening rides. Most trips were less than 100 miles, and my motorcycle ownership and learning curve was still in a steep ascent. For instance, when I had a flat tire, I learned how to take off the back wheel and roll it to a gas station where the inner tube could be patched. It was there I also learned to carry the tools necessary to skin the tire and how important it was to carry a tire pump and inner-tube patch kit.

As summer approached, I was faced with either riding in a bus back home to Montana from Indiana or riding my motorcycle. The first option was sweetened by my parents sending me enough money to purchase a bus ticket and food for the three-day trip. The second option meant I would have my motorcycle to ride for the summer. The downside to the second option was my parents would discover I had gone against their wishes, advice, and prohibition, and that I had bought a motorcycle.

One of my classmates lived along the route to home. Together we concocted a plan in which his parents and mine would send us the money we needed to purchase the bus tickets and food; then we'd pool the funds and ride the 305cc Honda home. I'd drop him off in Minnesota and go on alone. It would be my first long trip and a real adventure for both of us, far more than riding a bus, which held none of the allure of the open road.

Neither of us had the first clue about making a long ride on a motorcycle. We knew it could be done because we had seen other motorcyclists traveling though our small college town in Indiana, and we had read some magazine stories and advertisements about traveling. Our first major decision was how to ready the motorcycle for the long trip.

Since I owned the Honda and any upgrades or accessories would be mine, the costs would also be mine. As a poor college student, the budget for the upgrades and repairs had a fairly low ceiling. I saved a few dollars by learning how to change the oil, filter, and spark plug and stayed well away from the expensive Honda motorcycle shop.

A trip to the shop for more complicated repairs and advice was inevitable, however. While there, the shop owner suggested a handlebar-mounted windscreen, luggage rack, and leather saddlebags. That combination was a budget buster, so all I left with was a rear luggage rack.

While testing the Honda, I discovered why a windscreen had been suggested—a hailstorm ravaged my hands, face, and head worse than anything I had experienced at home. I bought the windscreen and the cheapest motorcycle helmet they offered with a bubble-like face shield. Brian and I decided we'd purchase any gloves, jackets, and saddlebags from the used army-surplus store.

We bought two backpacks to use as saddlebags. While not as stylish as the proffered leather saddlebags from the Honda dealer, they easily held more of our gear, and only cost $10 for the pair.

A test of our new gear and saddlebags proved that all the choices we had made were going to work. The windscreen kept wind off me, the helmet face shield prevented my face from being peppered by bugs, and the canvass saddlebags were easily mounted with their straps over the back of the seat. Our 2- to 3-mile test ride around town convinced us we were ready for the trip.

On the morning of departure we filled the saddle packs, one for each of us. We piled two 50- to 60-pound suitcases on the luggage rack. Then we found a pile of gear on the ground that had no place to go: blankets for sleeping and a small tent.

The dilemma was solved after an hour of trying to repack what we had by making a quick trip to the Harley-Davidson dealer. I purchased a 3- to 4-foot sissy bar that could be attached to the motorcycle frame and luggage rack with hose clamps and U-bolts.

Back at our starting point we attached the new sissy bar, repacked the saddle packs and luggage rack, and used rope to tie the tent and blankets onto the sissy bar. Looking at the loaded motorcycle from the side, everything looked like it had a home, except for one important aspect: there was no room on the back of the seat for Brian.

We repacked, this time strapping the blankets and tent to the back of the sissy bar and on top of the two suitcases, which left room for the rear passenger. We made several attempts to get Brian on the back of the Honda while I was holding it upright, but he could not wedge himself in between the sissy bar and my back. We finally solved this problem by having him sit on the motorcycle first, and while he held it upright, I climbed on the front. It was a tight fit, and I was hunched over the gas tank,, but I managed to start the motorcycle and we left town, only three hours behind schedule. We were on the road.

The trip lasted about 5 miles until a passing driver waved at us, gesturing frantically at our makeshift saddle packs—the backpacks we had bought were being ripped, and our clothes were leaking out of the pack behind us. The bags had been flopping near the rear wheel and the friction ripped open the canvass.

While Brian walked back toward town collecting our shoes, books, and clothes, I tried to use more rope to repair the torn bags and make a barrier that would keep the bags from hitting the rear wheel. The field repair was workable, but the pile attached to the sissy bar became higher and wider.

It was only a few hours until disaster struck.

We were wobbling along nicely at 50 to 60 miles per hour. It took more throttle than I anticipated, but I chose to ignore that sign, attributing it instead to strong headwinds. Another car pulled up next to us and the passenger pointed behind us. Thinking the saddle pack fix had failed, I slowed and looked behind us. Instead of the road and landscape receding, I saw only smoke, and at first I thought the saddle packs were on fire. When I pulled over and stopped, we got off the motorcycle and inspected the bags. There was no fire, and there were no singed parts. Where the smoke had come from was a mystery to us both.

We remounted and I tried to start the motorcycle. After several tries it started, but it took high revs and a slipping clutch to get rolling again. As soon as we were moving, I turned around again. Another huge cloud of gray smoke was covering the entire road. I knew then something was seriously wrong. Rather than stop, I decided to baby the wallowing Honda the next few miles to a fairly large town; the name escapes me now.

Once there, we slowly made our way to a Honda motorcycle shop. Lucky for us, the mechanic had enough time to make two diagnoses. First, he said we had burned a hole in a piston. Neither Brian nor I had a clue what that meant. The second diagnosis was I had worn the clutch plates down to nothing by slipping it to keep moving.

The bad news was that the motorcycle was nearly dead. The good news was the shop had the parts in stock needed to make the repairs. Even more good news was they could get the job done the next day, even though it was a Saturday. But then the bomb dropped—the cost of the parts and labor would consume nearly all of our travel funds.

After reviewing our budget, sleeping, and eating options, and the lies we could tell to explain how Brian hadn't made it to the bus depot on schedule, we told the shop to do the work. We carried our gear to an anonymous city park. We didn't have enough money for a cheap motel room, so it was camping under the stars for us.

Jail and Hookers

We didn't eat; it cost too much. What little money we had barely covered the gas needed to get Brian home. A quick collect call assured his parents that he was OK, that there had been a breakdown, and that he would be at the bus station a day later than planned.

That base covered, we set up camp in the city's downtown park, and it looked like things were going to work out until a local police officer in a patrol car rousted us after dark and told us we could not spend the night there.

The officer was a nice enough fellow, though, and while poking through our gear on the picnic table, he explained the park was only open during daylight hours and that we would have to move out. When we said we had no money for a room and that our motorcycle was being repaired, his demeanor changed. It was clear he had an opinion about motorcycles and motorcycle riders, and there was nothing two Quaker boys on a Honda could do to convince him we were not road trash drinking, raping, and pillaging our way through town. After much pleading and a few tears, he finally relented. "Well," he said, "you boys could sleep in our jail tonight."

He let us pack up all our gear and carry it over to the nearby city jail. Inside, we were told to take off our belts, strip out our shoelaces, and empty our pockets into a box. Our road and camping gear was stashed in a corner, and we were led through a couple of locked doors and into a cell. When the cell door was shut, my pal looked at me like I was the one who was responsible for our current situation.

The cell was the real thing. Neither of us had ever been jailed before, but the bunk bed was steel and lacked any mattress or blanket, and the stainless-steel toilet and sink gleamed in the dark from the pale light of the hallway. While I was trying to figure out if we had

Dressing in the proper riding attire included leather jacket, leather pants, heavy-duty engineer boots, and a riding cap. I am pictured here at the start of a weekend camping trip.

been arrested, Brian was talking to himself, imagining explaining to his mother and father how he had ended up in jail.

It was impossible to sleep on those steel bunks. Around 10 p.m., we were sitting on the lower bunk when the first load of working ladies were brought into the cell area and locked in a cell across from us. There were five or six of them, and they seemed to be having a good time, acting as if the bunks were a bar and the toilet a private table. They saw us from across two sets of bars, locked doors, and the open expanse of the hallway.

They began to ask us questions. Brian, thinking he was making new friends who might help us get out of jail, spilled his guts: we were motorcyclists, had no money, and our motorcycle was in a shop being repaired. The girls started to laugh, then make fun of us. We didn't know whether to laugh or cry. We were being cut up by a group of mini-skirt-clad, push-up-bra-wearing prostitutes. Many of them stood taller than us in their heels, and we could practically see their neon lipstick in the dark and taste their overbearing perfume. Another group of working ladies was soon brought in, and they were enlightened by the first group about who and what we were doing across from them.

By midnight the jail had become a party zone. The ladies were trying every way possible to embarrass us and to make fun at our expense. They showed us their bodies, their legs and asses and breasts, visions too scandalous for Brian, and he had to look away. When they could not get his attention with visual aids, they began throwing their underwear across the hall, trying to land it in our cell. Though Brian was uncomfortable, I was not. I'd take this over a Quaker headmaster any day. I think most people would.

The fun stopped when a jailer came back into the cells. "Shut up!" he yelled at the girls, trying to figure out what all the ladies' underwear was doing inside and outside our cell. His answer to the party scene was to turn on a radio loud and turn off all the lights for the night.

Sometime around dawn, the hookers were released. I later learned from the mechanic at the Honda shop that the Friday night had been "round up the hookers night," good income for all the bail bondsmen, the town court system, and a few arresting officers who were either rewarded for not busting the working ladies with either cash or dark-alley favors.

Around 9 a.m., Brian and I were released with the warning, "You trash should get out of town fast." All of our belongings were returned, and we stumbled from the jail and into the street, left to haul all our gear to the Honda shop.

I never did find out if we had been arrested, booked, or charged with anything. I can remember they took our fingerprints and wrote down our names and who to call in case of an emergency. Brian and I did supply our parents' telephone numbers, fearing they'd actually be used but too shocked by the predicament to lie or refuse to give them. When they handed back our shoelaces, I asked why they took them in the first place. "To keep from hanging yourselves," the officer said.

On the Road

We sat around the Honda shop until late afternoon when the motor repairs were finished, and we were relieved of nearly all our cash. Rather than spend another night in the town (and possibly the jail, dodging lacy bullets from a squadron of curvy sharpshooters), we decided to drive all night, again passing on any meals. The mechanic at the Honda shop was nice enough to buy us each a cola, share his sandwich, and wish us good luck.

The decision to drive all night was a mistake. First, with the full load we had on the motorcycle, the headlight was pointed about 45 degrees into the air, so I could not see any of the pavement in front of us. Second, trying to avoid blowing another hole in the piston, I chose to follow behind any slow trucks, following the glow of their crimson taillights. Several of the trucks spewed exhaust fumes bad enough to nearly blind me. Brian got sick, spewing the cola and sandwich we had for our late lunch all over the gravel of the shoulder.

The night turned to day, and still I did not want to go faster than 50 miles per hour. The motorcycle wobbled from one side of the lane to the other whenever I accelerated—not surprising when I look back on how much weight it was carrying and how poorly packed it was. The front tire was nearly off the pavement.

We got Brian to the Minneapolis bus station before dark. From there, it was just a few miles to his home in the Twin Cities. There was no money left in our pockets other than some change to call his parents. We offloaded his gear and he said he would try to borrow some money from either his mom or dad and sneak it to me in the back of the bus station parking lot where I was to hide; they didn't know he was on a motorcycle, much less had brought a friend along for the ride.

He never told me what story he sold to his parents, but he did come back to where I was parked with $20. He disappeared, and I rode out of town with a full tank of gas. Brian and I never spoke after that first trip. He never returned to the college, so the tale of how the $20 was secured has been left to speculation. Whatever it was, I think he paid a high price for it.

The rest of my first trip was uneventful, except for the night the manager of a truck stop and restaurant paid me $30 and all the food I could eat to wash dishes and clean the kitchen. After that truck-stop oasis, the trip was just droning miles of road, little food, and some water, and learning to be creative whenever I needed gas. I learned that some gas pumps, although turned off at night, had gas remaining in the hoses, and if the nozzle was unlocked, I could drain a little into my motorcycle tank when no one was watching. I also learned how to siphon gas out of lawnmowers that were left unattended, a trick a Harley-Davidson rider I met had taught me. I always left 25 cents on top of the empty mower when I used that method. While the outlaw Harley-Davidson owner also taught me how to siphon gas out of parked cars, I never had the courage to fill my tank this way.

Big Bike to Adventure

When I finished that first trip, I looked back and realized that while the Honda was a fine motorcycle for running around town or day rides, it was not what I thought I needed for extended travel. My motorcycle bad-boy friends kept telling me I needed a real motorcycle for travel, not what some of them called "Jap crap." Nonetheless, that trip had changed me. I was ready to move into the world of big bike travel and adventure.

Purchasing my first adventure trip motorcycle was an extremely difficult choice. My initial list of requirements was fluid because I was not firmly fixed on whether or not it would be used solely for travel on pavement or for some off-road, dirt-caked adventure.

Topping the list was the purchase price. I had been saving money by any means that I could, including doing some ugly, backbreaking firefighting, but the large coffee can for the motorcycle fund was far from overflowing. It was full of more coins than bills, money that would jingle in your pocket but not stack on your table. I vowed not to borrow any more money, so what was saved limited what could be spent.

Also on the list was a motorcycle that was simple. I still did not understand the electronic or mechanical systems of motorcycles as well as I knew I should. I knew how to change oil on my Honda or drain the carburetor on a lawnmower, but how a battery charged or how ignition points allowed spark to jump were mysteries.

Suspension, especially rear suspension, was also on the checklist. If I was going to pilot my motorcycle over some of the ranch roads around my home in Montana, I needed a sturdy suspension system to soften the potholes and washboard sections. I also had learned that carrying travel gear required a stiffer suspension than that of the Honda Super Hawk.

Regular gas—not the high-grade premium stuff—was another requirement. I knew I wouldn't be able to purchase high-octane gas in the remote mountain regions of Montana and Wyoming, and I needed a motorcycle that could function well on regular gas, the fuel farm tractors and some field-irrigation pumps used.

Carrying capacity was another prerequisite. The motorcycle had to be large enough to carry my sleeping bag, tent, cook stove, coffee pot, frying pan, ax, fishing pole, and clothes. That meant a luggage rack on the back as well as saddlebags, accessories I needed to budget for. No more backpacks for me.

Anticipating an occasional tip over or field repair, whichever motorcycle I bought I had to be able to pick up and fix myself, as I would be traveling alone. I knew my dreams of roaming the Rocky Mountains were grounded by the knowledge that sooner or later I'd have to make engine or tire repairs with the motorcycle lying on its side of those ancient cliffs. The same was true for more gentle landscapes. Sooner or later, I'd have to rock the bike from sand and mud, freeing the wheels so I could continue my journey, wherever it took me, wherever I was going.

As my search narrowed, a new item was added to my list of requirements: crash bars. Their dual functionality made sense. I knew I would

After rebuilding the engine and giving it a fresh paint job, the 1945 Indian was my type of touring motorcycle for several years.

want to rest my feet on top of the front crash bars while driving down a long paved road. The models I saw with the additional crash bars on the back seemed not only to protect the rear fender assembly and saddlebags, but they helped if one needed to roll the motorcycle upright after falling onto its side. One seller told me that that is why they are actually called roll bars, not crash bars.

Spare parts such as spark plugs and inner tubes were also on the checklist. As I asked about availability, I was told, "You can get a spark plug for this motorcycle at any car parts or farm equipment store in town." Others said, "You can order what you need in advance, because they have to come from Japan or Germany, but chances are you won't need anything because these foreign motorcycles don't break down." Right.

My search eventually ruled out the exotic and expensive foreign models. The dreams I had of my motorcycle parked on the shore of a pristine mountain lake with the campfire crackling while I reclined in front of my tent digesting a freshly caught trout and sipping a cup of coffee did not include an expensive bag of spare cables, spark plugs, and carburetor sliders resting in my saddlebags.

That same vision narrowed down the search even further to a motorcycle that could run if the battery was dead or the electric starter

I often return to some of the places my first motorcycle took me to fish, camp, cook dinner over an open fire, and watch the sun set. That's the Big Horn River in Montana, where the fish are still waiting for me, like the ones hanging from the stringer caught one afternoon. Unfortunately the mosquitoes and horse flies are still there too, waiting for my return.

failed. While I did not know how a magneto worked, the various sellers of used motorcycles convinced me that kick-starting a motorcycle with a dead battery but working magneto was far superior to hiking to the nearest town to rent a truck or purchase a new battery.

I bought a well-used 1945 Indian Chief found leaning against the back wall of a gas station in Cody, Wyoming. The former owner had used interior house paint to give it that custom shine and didn't miss an inch. He even splattered the seat and tires with it. It was ugly, but looked all the more wild for it, promising adventure in its discolored way. It featured a leaf-spring front end, buddy seat, and open exhaust pipe. The former owner had moved on to an English model with upgraded electrics and more speed. When I asked if the dead castaway ran, he said, "No, but it kinda did when it was parked there."

It took me several weeks to get it running, and then some test runs to work out the kinks, but within months my dream of being parked by a lake became a reality. Over the following spring and summer, I bounced and bumped over hundreds of miles of gravel roads, jeep trails, cow paths, and more, spending afternoons fishing, then evenings cooking over a small open fire before crawling into my sleeping bag and firing my gun skyward or into a tree trunk to ward off curious bears. My trips were no longer day trips. They were consuming Mondays and Fridays as well as the weekends in between.

I miss those times. I can almost taste the fresh-cooked trout. I even miss the mosquitoes and horse flies that made my morning ablutions a bug-swatting competition. The red welts on my skin told me I was alive. The first trip on the Honda had morphed into a perpetual adventure through the next years, and I moved from a weekender to a serious traveler. Losing my naiveté was something I missed but do not regret.

Most of all I miss that first motorcycle. The Chief cost just $25, but it was priceless to me, as valuable as the freedom of the road itself.

CHAPTER THREE

TWO-WHEELED CRACK

Casual Motorcyclist

A drug. Motorcycles had become a drug addiction by the time I returned to college. More important to me than girls or studying to become a physician, motorcycles moved to the top of my priorities list.

It was the era of peace and love, flower children, and rebelling against the system. My parents had decided to roll their prodigy dreams on to my younger brother, funneling their limited financial resources and attention in his direction rather than mine. Months went by with no contact with my family. I was comfortable being alone because I had developed a good circle of friends and had my motorcycle. When friends were unavailable, my motorcycle filled any void.

During this period there seemed to be enough money in the family coffers to see that my college tuition was paid for, but I needed to work at the college kitchen to pay for room and board. The books I needed came out of a small monthly allowance I received from my parents, who reasoned that funding my school and books exonerated them from any other financial help, and if I did not have any money, then I would not be paying for gasoline or parts for my motorcycle, or almost a bigger horror, dates with girls. They thought if I was broke I would stay in my room and study. Their plan worked for a few months, but then I discovered the buy-low-sell-high theorem.

Through one of my motorcycle friends, I learned that an 80-cubic-inch flathead Harley-Davidson was for sale. It was cheap because it did not run. I bought it, dragged it back to my dorm room, and took it apart. And after a month and some experiments, it ran. As soon as it was functional, I found a buyer who paid me far more than I had paid for the motorcycle and the parts. I made a handsome profit.

Next, I sold the car I was using, again for more than I had paid, and replaced it with one that was far cheaper. This second car I sold, again for a tidy profit. Then a 45-cubic-inch Harley-Davidson became available, which I also bought and sold. My life as a college student was slipping away as I learned how to profit from buying and selling used cars and motorcycles.

I was living in the college dorm, spending more time trying to make old motorcycles and cars run than on my studies, even though motor vehicles were prohibited on campus by both the Quaker authorities and my parents. To counter this, I rented an unheated garage off-campus to hide and store my various vehicles. I snuck parts into my dorm room and did the cleaning and hand work when I should have been studying. While the level of my mechanical skills was improving, my academic levels were dropping off.

One afternoon, some fellow students decided to have some fun with me. I had been washing motorcycle parts in my room using gasoline as the cleaner, smelling up the entire hallway. The fun-makers banged on my door and shouted that the school authorities were coming to shut me down. I quickly dumped the fuel out the

A 1948 Indian Chief project bike was converted to a chopper to give me a taste of the chopper lifestyle. I did not like the handling or the lack of protection. I sold the motorcycle and moved on to other motorcycle building and restoration projects. This was the last chopper I owned.

window and frantically tried to make my room look like a student's room and less like a mechanic's workshop.

Several hours went by and no authorities appeared, so I returned to cleaning motorcycle parts with a fresh supply of gas. The same students banged on my door again with the repeated warning, and I went through the earlier steps to sanitize my room. Again, no authorities showed, and again I went back to work.

The third time the merrymakers tried to disrupt my cleaning I came out of my room and chased them around the halls. They ducked into their rooms and locked their doors. The metal scraper I had been using to pick gasket pieces off a cylinder head had scared them. They thought the flat paint scraper was a knife. I did not even realize I had it in hand until the next day when I was hauled into the college authority office. I thought I was being summoned to explain my two cars and motorcycles in the school parking lot, or worse, the smell of gasoline in the dormitory hallway. Further down the list was my choice of off-campus friends who included no-account motorcyclists and car mechanics, long-haired free-love advocates who had a passion for smoking weed, and a couple of local girls who liked to drink, ride, and smoke, and often at the same time atop a screaming motorcycle.

I was interrogated by a surly school official. I was waiting for the shoe to drop about my vehicles, poor grades, or worse (the near toxic levels of flammables in my room). When I finally became tired of the line of questioning and was ready to plead guilty to the vehicle possession charge, I challenged him to get to the point, and he did.

He said it had been brought to his attention that I was spending time outside the Quaker life, that I had been seen off-campus and across the nearby state line in a bar drinking alcohol. He said that he had been contacted by my parents about my fraternizing with motorcyclists and my slipping academic levels. While not referring to it, it seemed he was going down a long list of items he felt were outside the parameters of what was acceptable at the Quaker college. At the top of the list were motorcycles and their reflection of rebellion. As I looked across his academic desk at his academic coat, his crumpled tie, and crisp white shirt, I thought to myself, "This guy has no clue. He hasn't mentioned my dope-smoking friends who make a few dollars on the side selling what they don't smoke, the guy who makes a living selling car parts he collects off parked cars, or the two guys I go fishing with who I think are draft dodgers."

He summed up his list of infringements in an almost fatherly fashion by saying, "We're worried about you. As I sit here looking at your hippie beads, long hair, black leather jacket, and obvious attitude, I don't see a future doctor in the making."

I found myself having to move my cars and motorcycles off campus while in college. Here my friend was towing my Harley-Davidson behind my car when the Harley refused to start one cold morning. I was trying to keep both vehicles away from the eyes of school authorities, who prohibited me from having motor vehicles on campus, but they had not ruled about owning one and parking it off campus.

The stern Quaker then asked why I had been reported as having wildly chased another student with a knife in my hand, and he wanted to know if it was true. The question was laughable, and I told him so. He asked me to explain, which I did. I pled guilty to chasing not one, but *several* students down the hallway. When I told him I had been cleaning motorcycle parts, I saw him wince.

He seemed to accept my guilty plea to chasing some irritating students away from my room while waving a paint scraper or large screwdriver at them. He pondered my punishment for a moment while staring at the ceiling. Finally, he said, "It's clear you have some problems here. Whether you are rebelling against our collegiate setting, the Quaker life, or your parents is unclear. If we are going to be able to help you, I need to know what you're rebelling against."

I remembered Marlon Brando in *The Wild One* and his line, that perfect and cool response. I gazed at the Quaker across the expanse of the desk during that cool afternoon so long ago.

From an early age, my hobby was fishing. While the second hobby, motorcycles, came into being in my teens, the fishing hobby never went away.

"What have you got?"

That response stalled whatever procedure he was planning to follow. He looked at me, and after all the questions and the drama, I was only chastised with the warning that I had better change, or change was going to be made for me. I was going to be carefully watched in the future, and then he told me to go back to my dorm where a dorm proctor kept me under an eagle eye for the next week. I shut down my dorm-room repair shop and was forced to spend nights moving my vehicles around the off-campus parking spots I had found. I was missing classes, juggling spare time to ride motorcycles to bars or to fishing spots, and dating girls while trying to make financial ends meet to support my motorcycle habit. Something was going to have to give.

One sunny afternoon, as I was looking through a microscope during a biology class, trying to draw a copy of the amoeba I was seeing, I heard the start of a friend's Norton Atlas engine. We had spent the evening before unsuccessfully trying to get it working. The sound of the Norton became quieter as he rode away, but it was the last straw that killed the dreams of my parents. I quit college the next day, dropped out, and tuned into my own world.

Over the next months, I managed to live by begging odd jobs, sleeping in the back of my car, and sponging showers and beds from my friends who lived on campus or in apartments near the campus. At one point all I had left was a nickel. I gave it to my girlfriend, saying, "Well, if I have to start dead broke, I might as well really start at zero."

The next day I called my parents—collect. When my father accepted the call from the operator, his first words were, "The school told us you had dropped out some weeks ago. If you were here, I'd beat you, you and that motorcycle. Here, talk to your mother."

He handed the telephone to Mom and I said, "Mom, I have quit college."

"Well, what are you going to do instead?" she asked. "We're not sending you any money. If you need money, sell that motorcycle of yours."

"Mom," I answered after a few seconds. "I'm going to ride my motorcycle. Maybe I'll go fishing too."

"Oh no," my mother answered, and then she hung up the phone.

That was the last time I spoke with my parents about my future for the next two or three years. I saw them briefly on a stop-over on the way to a summer job, but neither they nor I had anything to say to each other. Little was said other than a cordial hello and goodbye.

It was 1967, the Summer of Love. Near its end, I moved to the East Coast and did not call or speak with my parents for the next two years. They refused to talk to me when I tried to call them and hung up when they recognized my voice. I had been shunned for choosing

I discovered that a motorcycle could take me to places where the fishing was far better than where my cars or hiking could easily reach. Motorcycles and fishing morphed into a priority when education slipped off my personal goals.

My first new motorcycle was a 1968 BMW R69US. BMW was struggling that year, manufacturing about 5,000 bikes in the whole year. I was able to buy this motorcycle because my local dealer could not find a customer. I had to arrange financing; it was the first time I used credit. This motorcycle broadened my understanding of motorcycle travel and speed versus my previous experience with the 1945 Indian Chief. The BMW needed no repairs and was far quicker than my Indians or Harley-Davidsons.

a life where the number-one priority was motorcycles, number-two was money for my motorcycle, and number-three was a girlfriend who eventually became a wife, albeit for a short while.

The years ahead were devoted to as much motorcycling as possible. I sold the 1945 Indian and bought a new 1968 BMW R69US. I saw that many of the travelers I encountered were using BMW motorcycles, and though I loved my Indian, it constantly required maintenance. BMW owners convinced me daily attention wasn't necessary for their motorcycles, so I relented and bought German.

The R69US was the first new motorcycle I owned. Sometimes at night I rolled it up the stairs and into our living room, imagining my motorcycle was probably the only two-wheeler next to the couch inside any of the houses of Media, Pennsylvania. There it sat, when one day a man and his wife came to our apartment to purchase a refrigerator we were selling. He noted the BMW and said, "Nice motorcycle. Looks cool. I like the English stuff but have never seen one sitting in a living room. They leak too much oil and gas."

I soon found work as a stonemason's apprentice and common laborer for a man who owned a BSA motorcycle and several Hendersons. My motorcycle was my main transport to and from the job sites. Weekends would find me riding the BMW aimlessly, just happy to be moving through the wind on two wheels. Sometimes I attended hippie gatherings for the music offered, but most often it was to ride to and from the event and through the surrounding country-side. At one weekend musical jamboree, I spent more time walking

My BMW R69US had carried the two of us to a remote mountain lake where there was plenty of fish to catch.

through mud to check on my motorcycle than I did watching acts on the stage, the safety of the motorcycle being more important to me than the famed music stars of the stage.

My motorcycle was also a way for me to pursue my favorite hobby—fishing. From an early age, I liked to fish. Fishing was one of the few things my father and I did together.

I discovered that motorcycles were a way for me to catch more and bigger fish because I could use the motorcycles to reach places that were too far from good paved roads to drive a car. The off-road fishing trips became a challenge for me to test my off-pavement driving skills while at the same time pursuing my hobby.

Prior to 1970, I bought and sold several motorcycles, principally to make money. These projects gave me an opportunity to test different types of motorcycles while learning the mechanics necessary to keep them upright and running. Whether scouting for good deals on used motorcycles or buying parts, I had little time for personal relationships. Any friendships that I developed usually revolved around motorcycles.

In a BMW dealer's shop one weekend, I saw a poster on the wall with a picture of a man who had ridden his BMW motorcycle to Alaska and then down to the bottom of South America. I stood there looking at that poster, thinking, "Huh, a person could actually drive a motorcycle to Alaska and South America." A light had gone on inside my brain. I didn't know it then, but I think at some subconscious, unknowable level, I was already making plans to start roaming the earth by motorcycle.

CHAPTER FOUR

GOING ABROAD

My First Trip beyond North America

The BMW R69US carried me to Mexico and Canada, borders that were easy to cross at the time. The only proof of identification needed was a driver's license. While insurance may have been required, it was never asked for at the immigration or customs offices. I did several day trips into these neighboring countries.

With a BMW factory-fresh from Munich, I started my first trip off the North American continent with an R75/5.

I had been thinking about the pictures I had seen of the American on his BMW in Central and South America when my local BMW dealer told me I could purchase a new motorcycle through him and pick it up at BMW's headquarters in Munich, Germany. The purchase price would be less than what I would pay in the United States, and arrangements could be made for all the paperwork needed to travel in parts of Europe for a month, after which I could fly the motorcycle home. The idea stuck because I wanted to test my personal limits of riding well outside the borders of North America.

What sold me on the idea (and the bike) was not only would I acquire a newer model, but it also featured 150cc more displacement than my 600cc R69US. I sold the R69US and signed the necessary paperwork to collect a new BMW R75/5 in Munich during the summer of 1970. The BMW was black with white pinstripes on the sides, big and mean and loaded with chrome.

I had also decided to go back to college. I figured working with my head was going to be a better way to make enough money to pay for my motorcycle pursuits than working with my hands. Part of this decision was brought on by breaking several bones in my left hand while moving rocks at a job site. The broken bones and subsequent cast kept me off my motorcycle for several weeks, and I was forced to learn how to use the handlebar clutch with just two working fingers. I accepted an office job working with budgets and numbers while enrolling at a local university to study business.

A flight to London and an overnight train ride soon found me in Munich, however, collecting my new BMW R75/5. Over the next

In Spain, I fashioned a larger luggage rack to accommodate the additional traveling gear I added to allow cheaper travel by camping instead of staying in the more expensive hotels and guest houses. The welder (right) spoke no English and I spoke no Spanish, but we managed to overcome our language differences and get the job done with drawings and sign language.

After several weeks in Europe, the R75/5 had acquired numerous accessory additions for increasing carrying capacity and traveling at higher speeds on autobahns.

weeks I crossed from Germany and rode into France, Switzerland, Luxembourg, Italy, Spain, and Austria. The 10,000 miles introduced me to what I thought were perfect roads in the Alps, high-speed riding on autobahns, and European riding styles. Shipping the motorcycle from Europe back to the United States also introduced me to some of the less enjoyable but unavoidable bureaucratic paperwork associated with moving motorcycles across borders and water.

Once the BMW was in the United States, I began using it as my daily commuter, while at the same time applying the driving styles I had learned in Europe. This application included speed, which I felt capable of handling, but it was was not acceptable to local speed limits and drivers. I started to accumulate points on my driver's license.

One evening a friend with a Norton Commando challenged me to a race on a curving two-lane road. I was leading when we came

While I had graduated to BMWs as my choice for daily runners, I still had a thirst for Indian motorcycles. I once considered an Indian sidecar outfit but passed due to its slow speed and lack of maneuverability.

My need for speed needed some fine-tuning in my early days as I veered off the roadways and onto the racetracks. I bent or broke several frames, handlebars, and body parts while learning how to speed through curves.

After Stan Myers took me under his wing and started to teach me to use my head more and depend less on pure speed, I started to win races with my daily runner, the BMW R75/5.

around a left-hand curve into an oncoming car in my lane. The decision to drive off the road and into the dark unknown on the right side was the only option I had. I slammed into a telephone pole, screeching metal into the night.

The damage to the motorcycle was massive. I had hit the telephone pole head on, bending and smashing everything on the front end of the motorcycle. My body flew off the seat and into the pole, breaking some small bones in my left hand and fracturing my right arm. Also broken were my glasses, which I wore under my face shield. Luckily, my European learning had included wearing a motorcycle helmet, which probably saved my life. The helmet itself was cracked in half, a throw away, but it had done its job.

The next weeks were an awakening. While I healed, I realized that if I wanted to race or go fast on a motorcycle, then I should take that need for speed to racetracks, where at least all the traffic was moving in one direction. While the motorcycle was being repaired and my bones knitted back together, I began the process of acquiring a motorcycle racing license to road race the BMW in the Street Class category, a classification at the time for street-riding machines versus fully modified race machines.

For weekend racing, I often made changes to the bodywork on the BMW R75/5, entering it in up to three different classes. Sunday night would find me bolting touring parts back on and using the motorcycle until the next race to hunt new and exciting roads.

Gary Nixon, another entrant in my class, used the cylinder heads on my BMW to warm his hands before the race started at Bridgehampton, New York.

Stan Myers managed my skill level on the road-race tracks and improved the motorcycle handling and power to the point where I was racing in the open classes.

I also recognized that I had become a hunter of perfect roads, and what I wanted to find in the United States were motorcycling challenges as difficult as those I had found in the European Alps. Between a full school schedule and occasional roadracing weekends, I used my spare time to search for excellent motorcycling roads. I had become an addict, a junkie of speed and hardtop.

The next year was a wild mix of speed and road hunting. During the school weeks I commuted to work and the university on the BMW, and on weekends I toured to find more challenging terrain. Many weeks found me doing double duty on the motorcycle, taking off touring accessories and bolting on number plates, changing tires on a Friday night and then racing on Saturday and Sunday. Sunday evening would be spent driving back from the racetracks and changing the motorcycle back over for street riding the following week.

The first year of racing was difficult. I had much to learn. Over the winter between the first and second year, a BMW motorcycle dealer named Stan Myers stepped up and offered to assist me in my racing pursuits. He owned the second oldest BMW dealership in the United States and saw some potential in me as a motorcycle racer. We worked on my BMW to make it faster, as Myers helped me become more of a strategist and less a simple speed junkie.

I finally began winning in my second year. My street-legal BMW R75/5 did best in the street or production class racing, ideally suited for motorcycles similar to those any customer could purchase from a dealer. My technical skills, thanks to Myers' help, were vastly improved. While my BMW may not have been the fastest motorcycle in the class, I was able to make up for speed with all I had learned.

After graduating from BMW's mechanic training school, I was offered several opportunities to use the school's motorcycles and consult with its technical experts. I had also started to enter more advanced classes. The open class allowed more motorcycle modifications, resulting in higher speeds. My racing license graduated from that of a mere club racer to a professional category. We were racing nearly every weekend, from Canada to Ohio and along the East Coast.

In May 1973, I won the open production class race at Bridgehampton, New York. Stan Myers and I set our sights on a five-hour endurance race in September, a test for both the machine and its pilots. We prepared my R75/5 to the best of our limited budget and time, but decided to take along a spare motorcycle in case we needed parts. Stan had a well-used R75/5 that had been sitting underneath a tree over the winter. While it didn't run, it had all the spare mechanical parts we thought we might need during a five-hour endurance race. We named it the "Old Gray Dog."

The weekend was especially good for me. On Saturday I finished first in the 750cc café class and second in the open-street class. We changed tires and were ready for the five-hour race the next day, which required two riders. Our choice was well-known BMW racer Justus Taylor. I was to be the primary rider, while Taylor was to relieve me during the required breaks.

During the morning warmup laps, on the second lap, the rear wheel slid out as I was exiting a sharp turn, tossing the BMW and me down the track in a series of flip-flops. The fresh tires had not warmed up enough to wear off a hard outer coating. The crash was disastrous, seriously banging me up and totaling my BMW. When I returned to the pits, I told Myers and Taylor I was sorry, that the tire had just let go as I was coming out of a turn, and I had not been able to save it, that the weekend was over.

Myers looked at the Old Gray Dog and asked me if I still wanted to try to race. I told him I wanted to race but doubted I would do very well because of my injuries. Myers asked if my ego would take second

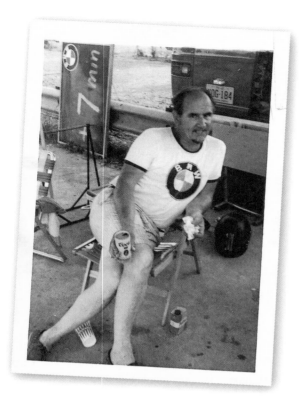

A happy Stan Myers enjoys a drink after our team won the five-hour endurance race in 1973 at Danville, Virginia. We had to use our backup parts motorcycle for the race, because I totaled my race bike earlier in the day. The sign in the background shows that at one point we had a seven-minute lead over second place.

place to being the first rider. It was an easy decision, as my ego was beaten out of me as I flip-flopped down the track an hour earlier.

Myers assigned each of us tasks to make the Old Gray Dog our race bike. We changed the oil, batteries, wheels, valves covers, mufflers, and the rear drive along with affixing number plates and safety wiring required nuts and bolts. In less than two hours we had the Gray Dog Running in time for Taylor to start the race.

Taylor did a magnificent job of keeping the Old Gray Dog near the front of the pack. When his time was up and he handed the motorcycle over to me, I could merely keep our place, too beat up to aggressively move ahead. We went back and forth until wear and tear took its toll on the other motorcycles and riders. Taylor moved into first place during the last leg of the race, and we came away as the winners.

That day gave me great confidence in BMWs. It also taught me to face adversity and look for ways around it, and be willing to let my ego take a back position to whatever the priority might be. That was a lesson I would need many times in the future when faced with bandits, jail, sickness, and mechanical breakdowns as I rode around the world. Motorcycle racing had added some valuable elements to my mental riding toolbox.

I was juggling a full class schedule at the university, a full-time job, and nearly full-time weekend racing. While the racing was rewarding from the standpoint of success, what was suffering was my wanderlust for hunting roads: my touring was limited to off-season.

Eventually I graduated with a business degree, changed jobs and locations, and stopped racing. My focus became setting aside enough money from my job to travel by motorcycle, hunting roads and exploring. My racing and mechanical skills encouraged me to go to places in Mexico, Canada, and Alaska, where other motorcyclists were seldom seen. Their lack of language skills and the uncertainty of their mechanical skills if faced with breakdowns kept them in the United States. My experience traveling in Europe with little or no language skills had taught me that language was not a barrier. As for the mechanical concerns regarding the motorcycle, racing had taught me how to be a fairly good mechanic. With respect to paperwork requirements for my motorcycle and me, again Europe had taught me to be flexible enough to cross borders. I felt that North America was mine, and that I could wander as far north and south as I wanted.

But it wasn't enough.

STAN MYERS PREPARED BMW WINS 5-HOUR ENDURANCE RACE AT DANVILLE, VIRGINIA.

Frazier hanging out on the "5 Hour" winning BMW.

AAMRR Road Races
Danville, Virginia
September 1-3, 1973

Wayne Frazier and Justus Taylor, well known BMW riders, won the 5-Hour Production Race on the BMW R75/5 sponsored by the Doylestown, Pennsylvania BMW dealer Stan Myers. Consistency and careful preparation payed off in this challenging event.

Danville was an especially good outing for Wayne since he also won the new 750cc Café Class and finished 2nd in the Open Street Class.

This BMW poster was sent to various media outlets in May 1973, showing we had scored a first-place finish in the Open Production Race.

This poster was sent to BMW dealers to show that we had a very successful weekend. Pictured is our winning "five-hour" machine, the Old Gray Dog, a parts bike that hadn't run for several years before we had to use it after I totaled my regular race bike during morning practice.

CHAPTER FIVE

FROM A STRAIGHT LINE TO A CIRCLE

Circumnavigating the Globe

A new job and the pursuit of advanced educational degrees found me well away from my favorite racetracks and sponsors. While I tried several times to make the cross-country drives necessary to meet racing schedules, time and money commitments found me choosing work and studies over racing.

I had been studying business and finance, and while looking at my own financial management, I came to the awakening that racing was far more expensive than I had realized. Reality set in when I realized I could ride motorcycles for weeks on the same budget I could spend preparing for a race, and even if I won, I might only come home with a trophy worth $5 to $10. I had to laugh at myself, knowing that my ego was telling me to keep throwing money into the deep, dark racing pit. Once I switched off the ego, I saw that racing was going to have to be moved down my list of priorities. It was simply not a rational return on investment.

Instead of merely spending money to ride roads, I listened to one of my university professors when he suggested we use our vacations to *make* money by recording them for sale in the form of travel or informational videos. An investment in recording equipment, some books, and classes on film making, and I thought I had found a way to pay for my off-road adventures.

Learning how to film was a new challenge. First I had to invest in some video equipment: camera, microphones, cables, and raw film. A couple of experiments proved my motorcycles were hard on cheap equipment, causing me to invest in more expensive equipment, and then a complete backup system if the first one failed, which happened on occasion.

Eventually I found some equipment that could withstand the bouncing and buffeting from being mounted on various motorcycles, as well withstand inclement weather and debris from the road. Although the system was heavy and blank tapes were bulky, all could be carried in one 30-pound package, leaving another 30 pounds for my riding gear and luggage.

In the mid-1980s, I set off to film the best roads around the world, circling North America first. I rode more than 20,000 miles, from Vermont to Georgia to California to Montana, and it resulted in the first in a series of films titled *Motorcycling on the Ten Best Highways in America*. With a long pit stop to learn about film editing, duplication, packaging, and marketing (and their associated costs), I felt I was ready to try some roads off the North American continent.

I worked my way around the globe: from North America to New Zealand, then Australia, and eventually across Europe and back to

Alpine Adventure Films
Presents

MOTORCYCLING ON THE TEN BEST HIGHWAYS IN AMERICA

MOTORCYCLING IN AMERICA

"*MOTORCYCLING ON THE TEN BEST HIGHWAYS IN AMERICA*" is a video "riders manual" on motorcycling on the best motorcycling roads in America. Included is information on where the best roads are, when they are open, riding conditions and tips for enjoying these roads on a motorcycle.

Alpine Adventure Films, P.O. Box 1598, Englewood, CO 80150-1598

This is the film cover for Best Highways in America, the first motorcycle travel film I made. I had much to learn about costs, equipment, and studio time.

Alpine Adventure Films
Presents

MOTORCYCLING ON THE TEN BEST HIGHWAYS IN THE ALPS

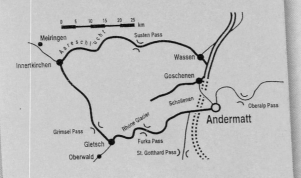

MOTORCYCLING IN THE ALPS

"MOTORCYCLING ON THE TEN BEST HIGHWAYS IN THE ALPS" is a video adventure about motorcycling on the best motorcycling roads in America. Known as "dream roads" the alpine highways by motorcycle are a lifetime adventure on the very best motorcycling roads in the world. This video gives the viewer maps, tips, riding secrets and an actual taste of riding in the Alps.

Alpine Adventure Films, P.O. Box 1598, Englewood, CO 80150-1598

I used a 1986 BMW K100RT as the film bike for Motorcycling on the Ten Best Highways in the Alps. I mounted the camera on the gas tank and shot through a hole in the wind screen.

A BMW R80G/S served as the film motorcycle for How to Motorcycle in Mexico. This film was more of a "how-to" film than my previous projects.

Alpine Adventure Films
Presents

HOW TO MOTORCYCLE IN MEXICO

MOTORCYCLING IN MEXICO

"HOW TO MOTORCYCLE IN MEXICO" is a video "riders manual" on motorcycling in Mexico. Included is information for motorcyclists on road conditions, Mexican entrance requirements and general riding conditions in Mexico.

Alpine Adventure Films, P.O. Box 1598, Englewood, CO 80150-1598 the United States. It was a wandering route, far from a straight line, and twice I had to stop, store equipment, return to the United States to edit film, deal with marketing problems, replenish my cash reserves, and then return to where my road gear was stored and continue to the next point.

The route around the world, once the dots were connected, was from east to west, starting in Denver, Colorado, and eventually returning there as my start point. I referred to that loop around the globe as my "I got lost" global romp, or "Four points far from a straight ride." It had taken nearly four years and required the use of four different motorcycles (two BMWs, a Yamaha, and a Kawasaki). When all was said and done, I had produced four films on motorcycle travel. While sales were slow, they were enough to support additional films about riding motorcycles in Alaska and keep in touch with other 'round-the-world travelers I had met while circling the globe.

I continued to travel when I could, seeking good roads in the western part of the United States, Canada, and Mexico. North in Alaska and south in Mexico, I often found myself well off paved roadways, exploring out-of-the way places that required honing my gravel or dirt-riding skills. These secondary routes also gave me an opportunity to try catching fish.

That first ride around the world was unplanned as a global loop. I set out to reach places by motorcycle just to ride and film the roads I knew to be good motorcycling roads. That had been one of the themes of my motorcycling life at that point.

In 1970, when I had flown to Europe and purchased the new BMW R75/5 motorcycle to hunt roads in the Alps and Pyrenees, I encountered what many other motorcyclists considered to be the best roads in the world. In the 1980s, there was enough time and money to chase rumors of other good motorcycling roads on the globe. After nearly four years, I had managed to bag what I had been told were superb motorcycling roads in North and Central America, Europe, Australia, and New Zealand. Along the way my route took me into parts of Africa and Asia, but more as a tourist and less as an adventuring rider.

When I returned to the United States and was sitting around one night with a well-traveled film producer, we were following my route on a globe when he said, "You know, while you were out there, you actually rode completely around the world." That was a surprise to me, because that had not been the goal, nowhere near a fixed program. As a motorcyclist who liked to ride good roads, and often fast, it had been my plan to seek out the best on the planet, not follow some circumscribed route. Numerous times I backtracked to re-ride exceptionally good roads, and twice had to make extended pit stops to deal with educational and job requirements, but returned to my stop points and continued forward. It wasn't easy to juggle a riding life with graduate school, teaching stints, and corporate managerial positions, and I knew I'd have to make a choice sooner or later.

At the end of that four-year expedition, I realized something had changed. While I would occasionally return to racetracks for special events, my lust for racing had diminished, while my dreams had become more focused on travel to faraway places. During that period, I took stock in what I had learned while producing films and came to a few conclusions:

- The amount of work it took to research and write a "how-to" or educational film was at least equal to the amount of time it had taken me to write earlier books on unrelated topics.
- Transporting motorcycles across water was expensive and time consuming and sometimes impossible due to bureaucratic paperwork. The costs associated with using only one motorcycle to film was financial foolishness.
- A motorcycle was merely a mechanical tool for exploration, and there was no reason to believe I had to carry or ship that tool over expanses of water when quality tools were available locally.
- Shipping motorcycles consumes a considerable amount of time, whether by air or water. I had to wait for a variety of out-of-country offices to open, purchase insurance, maintain and update other bureaucratic paperwork to cross borders, and deal with expected costs for hotels and supplies. Maybe more costly was the mental and physical strain to see every facet of shipping overseas through to the end.
- While my driving skills, both on and off pavement, were average or above, there were always faster and better local drivers, and I should not try to match their speeds or skills while traveling. My goal was to get from point A to point B, and I had no need to be the first to do so. Staying healthy was more important.
- Traveling alone gave me a greater opportunity to experience the environment I was passing through, making the trip *my* trip or journey, not *our* trip or journey.
- When traveling abroad and alone, there's always an element of danger with new and unexplored places and cultures. On my worldwide tour, I had seen death and carnage wrought upon motorcycle riders, some caused by themselves and some caused by elements beyond their control. There was a certain amount of courage needed to go certain places that were known to be unsafe. My conclusion was the element of courage was nothing more than

the suppressing of natural impulses. Flight was one of the most irresistible of these impulses, and it took courage to suppress. So I had to embrace death, and once doing so, become free of it. Danger, fear, and courage were all elements I had faced when racing motorcycles. If I were going to be adventuresome and go places outside my security zone, I had to apply some of the lessons I had learned from racing.

While I was marketing my videos, several motorcycle magazine editors and publishers asked me to submit articles for their publications about where I had been and what I had seen, and offer some tips about the country or reflections on the culture I was passing through. In lieu of payment, some magazines offered free advertising for my products. Others offered compensation that ranged from a few dollars to substantial amounts. A new source of income had presented itself as a way to pay for some of my motorcycle travel costs.

I didn't provide photographs with my first submissions. Because my travel around the world had been to shoot film, not photos, most of my gear was devoted to bulky video equipment. I seldom carried even simple cameras. While some editors purchased stock pictures for

AUSTRALIA & NEW ZEALAND

AUSTRALIA AND NEW ZEALAND BY MOTORCYCLE ($24.95 plus $5.00 S/H)
A 60-minute documentary about motorcycling in Australia and New Zealand. Filmed from atop motorcycles, this video, **MOTORCYCLING DOWN UNDER – NEW ZEALAND AND AUSTRALIA**, was produced to give the viewer a motorcycling video and audio experience of "OZ" and New Zealand. From Fraser Island to the Australian outback, Australia offers a wide variety of riding adventure for the motorcyclist. Tasmanian devils, bull dust and left side of the road riding are all reflected in this video adventure of Australia. In New Zealand the viewer is treated to adventures ranging from a ride on 90-Mile Beach, the jungles of the North Island and the Southern Alps of the South Island.

Due to the extreme distance from the United States to New Zealand and Australia, I shot both in a single film, using different motorcycles in both locations. I later folded some of the script from the New Zealand portion into a book about touring Kiwi country.

my articles, others were more adamant in their requirements. They wanted words and photographs.

This started an interesting chain of events. I took stock in what I was selling in the form of videos, which was principally information. My market for the films was much smaller than the potential market for magazine articles. A further market emerged when a publisher suggested I write a book, as long as I accompanied the text with photos.

My first years as a motorcycle journalist were lean. I sold a few articles to motorcycle travel magazines, and one took me on as a columnist. I wrote the book *Motorcycle Sex, or Freud Would Never Understand the Relationship between Me and My Motorcycle*, and it sold well enough to have the publisher invite me to write a second.

Soon I had three sources of income resulting from my travel around the globe: books, magazine articles, and films. Although the combined three were not enough to support a lifestyle of sustained, perpetual adventuring, they did suggest the potential for limited financial assistance.

The books sold well enough that I decided to move from the smaller markets to larger ones to breach larger motorcycle publications such as *Motorcyclist*, *Cycle World*, *Motorrad*, and *Easy Rider*. I proposed a larger article to a major American motorcycle publication, knowing that it paid far more to freelancers than any other magazines I had been dealing with up to that point. The editor knew me from *Motorcycle Sex* and some other articles I had written about travel and racing in smaller publications.

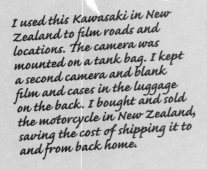

I used this Kawasaki in New Zealand to film roads and locations. The camera was mounted on a tank bag. I kept a second camera and blank film and cases in the luggage on the back. I bought and sold the motorcycle in New Zealand, saving the cost of shipping it to and from back home.

In Australia, I purchased a Yamaha XT600 in-country for the film. It carried me and the film equipment around the outer ring of Australia, through the middle, and then over to Tasmania and back. It was sold for nearly the same as the purchase price. Due to the stiff suspension, I was unable to use a considerable amount of the rough footage due to vibration of the camera, which also caused the first of the two cameras to virtually self-destruct.

After submitting my proposal to the editor for an article about traveling to Pamplona, Spain, by motorcycle from Germany, then spending four days camping with other motorcycle travelers, and running each morning with the bulls during the annual craziness of the celebration of Saint Fermin, I received a rather disheartening letter back declining my proposal. While the rejection letter was not a form letter, it did specifically say that the editor had previously seen my photographs in some other articles and that in his opinion my photographs were beneath his magazine's level of professionalism. To this, he added that I was no Hemingway, who had *also* written about Pamplona. When I explained in my response that Hemingway had not run with the bulls, as I was proposing, nor had he a single photograph in his Pulitzer and Nobel Prize–winning story about an old man and a fish, I received no further answer.

I traveled to Pamplona anyway and spent four mornings being trampled by other runners as well as by at least one bull in lieu of it all. I was able, however, to ride my motorcycle to and from the event and came away with a great adventure tale that ranged from sleeping in the city park to having seat cushions thrown at me for running too fast ahead of the bulls to arrive in the stadium unscathed.

While riding through Europe to and from Pamplona, I was still miffed by the editor's response. His response to my neophyte proposal seemed not only arrogant, but one that discouraged my future

This motorcycle passed me at speed while filming in Europe. At first I wanted to stay with it because it was moving in and out of traffic with what I thought was great skill. Common sense overruled my ego, however, for trying to capture daring footage on the road. Several miles after I slowed down, I passed the crashed motorcycle on the side of the road. I was told the cause was not pilot error but an oncoming car.

journalistic pursuits. But I realized the barrier to selling an article to his magazine was not the writing side but the photographic one. I would have to develop the skills of a photographer to sell my words.

Armed with a few boxes of my photographs and slides, I contacted a friend who worked for *Motorrad*, the largest motorcycle magazine in the world, and asked if he could introduce me to someone in their art department to critique my photography and I ended up spending several hours with the art director. At the end he said, "You have composition figured out, a natural talent, something we cannot easily teach many people. My recommendation to you is to shoot lots, give the magazine art department a wide selection to choose from, and let them do their jobs."

As a final suggestion, he told me not to spend thousands of dollars on photographic equipment. Instead, he recommended that I purchase a camera with a top-quality lens and not be sucked into paying many times more for just a brand name. This way, I could afford to purchase one camera for my primary camera and a second for backup if something happened to the first. I took his advice, invested in two cameras, a couple of lenses, and some supporting equipment. I also signed up for an inexpensive course in basic photography at a small university in Denver and learned the basics of having slides and photographs developed.

I kept traveling, using my cameras and plenty of film and discarding the heavier video equipment. A year later, I had another adventure article idea and submitted a proposal to *Motorcyclist*, a competing magazine to the one the earlier editor had worked for. I also submitted some samples of my photography. The *Motorcyclist* editor accepted my proposal and later published an article about carpel tunnel syndrome and motorcycle handlebars. Over the next years I sold articles and photographs to the some of the world's biggest and best motorcycling magazines, several times having my photographs used as cover photographs. One fishing magazine even paid me for a full-page use of one of my photographs with a motorcycle and string of fish hanging from it from a brown trout expedition near the Bighorn River in Montana. I did, however, promise myself never to submit a proposal or article to that first editor who turned me down.

For the next years (1980s) my work increased as an author and motorcycle journalist, while my interest in my regular job as a manager and my educational pursuits waned. Income from films, articles, and book sales was increasing, but not enough to make motorcycle travel and adventuring financially sustaining. Had it not been for the income from my regular job, I would not have been able to afford my continued adventures around the globe.

A second ride around the world in the late 1990s was the result of meeting a German book collector and self-proclaimed expert on global motorcycle rides. While he had never made one himself, he purported to be the world's leading expert on "'round-the-world motorcycle

While I had several close calls with road carnage, I luckily avoided any serious mishaps on my first trip around the world. To reduce engine and wind vibration while filming, I was forced to drive a little slower, but I also took it easy because of my unfamiliarity with those roads.

On the island of Tasmania, I thought some film footage along a beach would make good viewing. When I ran out of beach, I had to turn around or try riding through the bush. I took this photo after I hit an unseen rock that broke two of my toes and cracked the engine case, causing all the oil to drain out. That night I learned how to set the bones in my broken toes with Aussie pain killer—a good supply of beer.

touring." After he questioned me about my first global loop, he said, "You couldn't have made a ride around the world. I didn't know about it and you had no plan when you set off." At the time he was trying to market himself as a consultant to would-be motorcycle globe riders and was attempting to publish a book related to the matter.

I paid him little heed, in part because he had never done much long riding himself (much less alone) and I really did not care what he thought, said, or wrote about my accomplishments. As far as I was concerned, if he could not pass me on a racetrack, he had little standing in my motorcycling circle of friends. Others told me he was little more than an armchair rider, and several American and German journalists I knew placed him in the category of "nutter" or worse.

When I specifically asked him about how he could certify or validate my earlier ride around the world, he said I merely had to tell him what my route was and when I had done it, and he would post the information on his website, thereby validating my global loop. I studied his site and asked him if that was what others had done: merely told him of their claims. He said some had, while other stories he posted from books or articles he had read. The research for validating his claims was baseless; there was no way to validate the source, rendering his website and potential book as a mere collection of tales, some tall, others true. I could see no advantage in giving him free information for either his website or his alleged book. But it did bother me that he thought that to make a ride around the world, the rider needed a plan. When I contacted the people at Guinness World Records, they too said I needed a plan and sent me their "guidelines."

While I was not interested in a Guinness Record, knowing they passed out records for feats such as eating the most worms or standing on your head and other such foolishness, I did decide to make a long ride around the world, closely following some of their rules: I had to cover at least 16,000 net miles with no backtracking. "Easy," I thought. I planned to ride to the northernmost and southernmost points on the globe I could reach by road: Prudhoe Bay, Alaska; Ushuaia, Argentina; Cape Agulhas, South Africa; North Cape, Norway; and a side trip to Bluff, New Zealand. I called this my "Ride to the Ends of the Earth." When it was over, I had reached my touch points, crossed the equator four times, wore out a couple of motorcycles, and burned through a large stack of money. Now I felt I could hold my head up and give the self-proclaimed German expert the one finger while he read of my adventure. Later he wrote me, saying since I had again not provided him with the specific details of my ride, he couldn't verify that I had done it. What I suspected he was doing was looking for more fodder for his next book, and I decided I would save it for mine.

I was unscathed on the morning of the first day, ready to run with the bulls in Pamplona, Spain, during the annual celebration of Saint Fermin. After four mornings I was smiling less, having been run over by fellow runners and rolled on by one large bull. I had ridden my motorcycle for two days to arrive at the event, never really thinking about what would happen if I had not been able to ride back to my start point in Germany. The adventure taught me to make a Plan B in case my being alone brought a halt to my motorcycle travels. It also eventually taught me to learn to take and sell photographs.

CHAPTER SIX

TURNING PRO

A Passion Becomes a Profession

The second ride around the globe began in 1997 and started with a formal plan: to tag the ends of the earth. It also had some fixed timelines due to the need to purchase airline tickets for myself and to book shipping for my motorcycle. It was also based in part by that picture I had seen years earlier with the BMW rider in South America, and then later learning that he had also ridden through Africa and Europe. If he could do it, why couldn't I? Why couldn't anybody?

The easiest leg was another ride to Alaska. I had made numerous trips before, even leading motorcycle tours from Denver to the Arctic Circle and back. After one of those tours, I became tired of answering letters and telephone calls about what time of the year was best, what the road conditions were like, which gear to bring, which tires to use, where to sleep, how to avoid bears, and which motorcycle was the best. I collectively gathered all the information and convinced a publishing company to print a book titled *Alaska by Motorcycle*. At the same time I managed to produce another video titled *Motorcycling to Alaska*.

From Alaska I turned south, stopped in Denver long enough to edit the book and update the film, and then headed to the bottom of South America, a continent I'd never been to before. From South America my travels took me to the Republic of South Africa and then to the North Cape in Norway, on top of the world. The most difficult part of the entire journey was to ship the motorcycle from one point to another across huge expanses of water. Some creative work with number and lettering stamps and disassembling and then reassembling the motorcycle after having shipped it in parts into countries over a period of time solved two of the problems. The timing of parts arrivals at different destinations via air and sea cargo to coincide with my own arrival was tricky and resulted in some downtime when boxes of parts were delayed by customs or shipper problems, but eventually

Both motorcycle and rider fresh for a ride around the world. By this time, the BMW already had well over 150,000 miles on it.

I had learned that the BMW did not cross water well, unless on a bridge or boat. Here I saved several hundred miles by ferrying the disassembled G/S across a river.

all the parts came together and the old motorcycle was made almost new again.

After Europe, it was back to New Zealand while the motorcycle and parts moved eastward and eventually ended up back in the United States. While I was in New Zealand, I collected information on riding there and wrote another book on that part of the world. From New Zealand it was back to the United States, collecting my well-traveled motorcycle and concluding the end of a second trip around the globe.

I was much more savvy about international touring during my second ride around the world. I was selling more articles to magazines and book sales were increasing. Of course, the production costs associated with the books and films were *also* increasing, as I spent more time on the road and away from my office writing, scripting, editing, and marketing my products.

I was also learning some of the pluses and minuses of seeking out and having sponsors. Sometimes the effort put into securing a sponsor was far more than the return on the invested time, which could more profitably be spent writing articles or working on book or film projects. I spent 50 to 100 hours with one sponsor, Acerbis, answering letters (this was before e-mail had entered my world) and questions about how much coverage the sponsor would receive, where it would be placed, and how its product would be pictured—all for a product

The heavily laden R80G/S did not do well in soft sugar sand. Nor did it like mud, snow, or ice.

After the ride around the world, both the motorcycle and pilot were tired and worn down.

I could have purchased for $200 to $300. Another tire company, Metzler, agreed to provide me with free tires for my motorcycles, but would only ship them all to my home base of Denver. From there, I was responsible for the shipping costs, plus importation paperwork, to have the tires waiting for me at the places on the planet where I thought I would need them. Sometimes the costs associated with shipping and paperwork were twice the cost of the tire. While the tires were good products, the end result was going to be far more expensive than my local purchases combined with the possibility of shipping delays or importation hassles.

Again I was faced with the high price of shipping my motorcycle across oceans or over areas where I could neither secure visas for myself (such as Angola or Algeria) nor importation approvals without expensive handlers and paperwork such as a *Carnet de Passage*, a bond that allows you to sell a vehicle without paying customs tax on

The plaque describing the retired R80G/S tells only part of the story of the hard life this motorcycle had lived prior to, during, and after its ride around the world.

1981
BMW R80 G/S (modified)
Dr. Greg Frazier's GLOBE TROTTING MOTORCYCLE

Engine Size: 800cc
Power: 50 hp @ 6500 rpm
Speed: 168 kph / 103 mph

Features:
Long suspension, 21inch front wheel, Monolever rear swing arm, high exhaust, kick starter.

Accessories:
44-liter plastic tank, aluminum panniers, Harro tank bag, Aerostitch tank panniers, reinforced sub frame, Fox shock, Acerbis hand guards, Luftmeister windscreen (modified), Honda Goldwing seat (modified), Progressive Suspension fork springs, Motorrad Electric diode board, high-output regulator, gel-cell battery, dog skull.

The R80G/S was BMW's first modern production motorcycle reflecting its long involvement with *Gelaendesport* (GS), or off-road sport. Its immediate roots lay in the company's late-1970s successes in the African *Paris-Dakar* rally. Production versions of the rugged G/S proved well mannered both on and off road, and opened exciting new doors to adventurous motorcycle riders.

This R80G/S was ridden by professional motorcycle adventurer Dr. Gregory Frazier. A cult hero in the world-adventure motorcycle community, Frazier circumnavigated the globe five times by motorcycle, set race records on Pikes Peak, and writes informative, entertaining books and articles on motorcycling. This motorcycle accumulated over 240,000 miles, has been crashed numerous times. Every part has been repaired or replaced except the main bearings, drive shaft, and oil pump.

I donated the 'round-the-world R80G/S to Bob's BMW Museum in Jessup, Maryland. I was told they had drained all the oil out to keep it from leaving spots wherever it was parked.

Bob Henig (left), the author (middle), and riding pal Richard Livermore (right) trade tall tales about the 'round-the-world R80G/S on display at Bob's BMW Museum. I could almost hear the motorcycle groan when I suggested that it still had another long ride in it.

it. The deposits required for entry to a country for my BMW were often as much as five or six times the price of the motorcycle. I skipped those countries. In other instances I dismantled the motorcycle and shipped it in parts, then reassembled it upon arrival. One trick that I learned the expensive way was not to ship all the motorcycle parts at one time, even if they're in separate packages or crates; customs officials were wise enough to figure that although the parts were used, and thus taxed at a lower rate, the sum of the parts equaled one complete motorcycle and taxed it at the higher rate.

A significant lesson I learned before that second trip was I could no longer work at a steady job, take a leave of absence, and delegate my responsibilities to underlings. It was an expensive lesson that taught me the truth in "the buck stops here," which was in my case in my lap. Those "delegated responsibilities" could engage in a wide range of nefarious activities when I was not paying attention, but I was the one ultimately responsible as the manager.

I made some tough choices to secure the necessary time to travel and also to lessen my personal responsibilities. I needed the freedom to circle the globe without an ax hanging over my neck. My first decision was to go it alone without the financial security of paid vacations, expense accounts, and all the other ideas of security that come with a full-time job. I severely cut my personal overhead by changing my lifestyle. Gone was the mortgage on a house. I also quit buying newer cars, knowing I wouldn't need a car while I was on the road. Luxury items were no longer necessary either. I also became more judicious in managing time spent on hobbies versus time spent on money-making projects such as writing, editing, and marketing. I also divested myself of several volunteer projects. My focus became motorcycles first, income generation second, and fishing third. Personal relationships and the prospect of marriage and children had never been further away.

The second ride around the world did not stick to the plan, if there ever was one. While I began with what I thought was an adequate budget, by the halfway point in Africa, I realized it was just half of what I needed. If I was to continue from Tanzania north to the top of Norway, I was going to be pushing my BMW and eating sand. I made an unscheduled pit stop in my plan, flew back to the United States, and sold off enough of my assets, books, films, and magazine articles to bank enough money to get back onto my original route and finish my circle of the globe.

Upon the completion of that second ride around the world, I wrote two more books, produced another film, and started working part time as a copywriter and occasional event promoter. A motorcycle-magazine publisher offered me a full-time job as an editor; it would

This is the film cover from my second 'round-the-world ride using the BMW R80G/S. The film sold well enough to cover production costs and some of the ride itself. Long out of stock, it has become a classic on 'round-the-world riding.

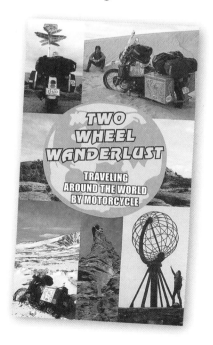

After completing my second ride around the globe, I felt I had conquered the world. In reality, I knew that many others had done what I had.

have been interesting, but it was too far away from home and tied me to an office, staff, and publication schedules. I passed on the editor job and several others that were offered in the loosely defined world of consultancy and decided to focus on seeking adventure and hunting interesting roads and places on two wheels.

The BMW R80G/S was tired. It had seen not only a hard global loop, but also numerous trips to Alaska and Mexico. I told people that when I walked by it in my studio I could hear it groan, almost see it shrivel if I looked at it. With at least 240,000 miles on it, everything had been smashed, replaced, bent, twisted, rebuilt, welded, and even held together with hose clamps. Even the motor and frame numbers had been "adjusted" over time to meet paperwork requirements that sometimes needed odd numbers to cross borders, or a number that matched a different R80G/S that I owned with a different registration. It leaked oil from numerous bolts and seals. The only bearings I had not replaced were the main and rod bearings. I wanted to see how long they would last. On the upside, it still ran when the battery was fresh.

Bob Henig, owner of Bob's BMW in Jessup, Maryland, once stopped at my studio. While looking at my collection of motorcycles, he asked if I would like to donate my tired motorcycle to his museum.

I laughed and said, "Why not?" It still stands there today as part of his rotating collection of BMWs.

The Next Ride

A year passed, and with my writing I had banked enough money for what I thought could be another ride around the world. This time I knew to make a more conservative budget and then double that to ensure me not having to make another extended and expensive pit stop.

After a winter of looking at maps of the world and researching what countries I could pass through without costing significant time, money, and energy, the plan began to come together. I was going to ride a motorcycle manufactured on the continent I was going to cross as I worked my way around the globe from west to east. In 2000, I started on my third ride around the world, crossing the United States on my 1947 Indian Chief. I left it in the United States at my studio in Denver while I flew with all my riding gear to Sao Paulo, South America, where I borrowed an Amazonas to explore the middle of that continent, west of the Andes and through the jungles of the Amazon. Since I had previously been down the west coast and up the east coast, I had no interest in following that route again.

I left Brazil and flew on to Europe where I used a BMW to cross as much of Europe as I could and stopped in Turkey. From there, I was halted by the inability to secure a transit visa, but I was also leaving the European continent and entering Asia.

I flew to Delhi, India, where I purchased a new Enfield 500. I spent the next months wandering India, Nepal, Sikkum, and Bangladesh. My

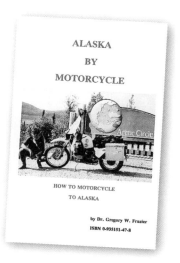

ALASKA
BY
MOTORCYCLE

HOW TO MOTORCYCLE
TO ALASKA

by Dr. Gregory W. Frazier
ISBN 0-935151-47-8

The R80G/S had made several trips to Alaska before starting on the trip around the world. It was on the second odometer when this photograph was taken, at an estimated 170,000 miles.

While the Copper Canyon was deeper and larger than America's Grand Canyon, it was far less spectacular. The main road in and out was about 40 miles and well traveled.

The road into and out of the Copper Canyon was gravel and not much of a challenge. A friend had taken the same road before on his fully loaded Harley-Davidson.

plan was loose. I knew I'd be halted trying to leave Nepal to the north and enter China and the eastern roads into Bhutan or Burma. I also had agreed to guide a woman who was seeking a Guinness World Record across India, so I ended up making a large circle around this part of Asia as I lead her through countries she was afraid to travel in alone.

After I guided the record-seeker close to the Pakistan border, I reversed my direction and rode back to Delhi, where I sold the

Enfield. I loaded myself and my travel gear onto an airplane and flew to Bangkok, then rode on an overnight train to Chiang Mai, where I used a 250cc Honda to loop around the north of Thailand. Due to paperwork requirements, I did not try to enter Laos or Cambodia, but instead returned the Honda to Chiang Mai and again flew with my riding gear and luggage to Taiwan, where I used a Taiwanese Hartford and SYM motorcycle to circle that island.

My plan had been to cross Asia on a motorcycle made on that continent. Rather than using one model, I used four, all manufactured in Asia, still moving from west to east. My favorite was the 500cc Enfield Bullet. It was a big bike for India, Nepal, Sikkum, and

I got tired of riding the paved roads through Central America and decided to try some jungle riding, which lasted for about 15 minutes until the road became a path that became a waterfall. This was my camping site for one night.

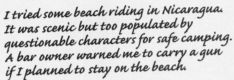

I purchased most of my meals at popular street markets such as this one in Guatemala.

I tried some beach riding in Nicaragua. It was scenic but too populated by questionable characters for safe camping. A bar owner warned me to carry a gun if I planned to stay on the beach.

Bangladesh, and funky enough to be interesting for me. I bought it new in Delhi from an Enfield dealer, who provided the fake paperwork I needed to get it licensed. While traveling through India, I stopped and made a tour of the Enfield factory in Jaipur, which for a motorhead like myself made the motorcycle more interesting. The other models I used were OK but bland. The Enfield had real character.

I skipped Australia and Antarctica because I never found a motorcycle that had been mass-produced in either place. I had found several that were custom-built in Australia, but none that were for sale to the general public.

I flew from Taiwan back to the United States, where I had been promised one of the new Indian motorcycles to complete the U.S. leg of my global loop, but that deal fell through as the company was in legal limbo when I returned. An offer surfaced for me to use a new 2000 model-year Harley-Davidson Ultra Classic though, and with it

I purchased a roadside snack at one of many stalls selling fresh fruit. Although my Spanish was limited, it seemed I could always negotiate a deal.

Sport bikes were the choice of locals. The only endurance- or adventure-style motorcycles I saw throughout Central America were being used by foreign travelers like myself.

I finished connecting the dots around the globe. I had crossed all 24 times zones from west to east.

While I had been on the road, book and film sales had done well. I had also sold enough articles and columns to magazines to keep a positive balance in my bank account and pay off my credit cards. Some investments I had made years earlier had moved out of the red and into the black. My net balance from the third ride around the world proved to me that if I managed my income responsibly, I could make a go of writing and riding.

Sometimes the road was good, other times, especially after rains, not so good. Twice I had to wait for a day until road crews could clean up mudslides like this one.

One of my rules for travel, anywhere, is not to drive at night. After dark I would not have been able to see either the rock or the donkey.

I went back to work on a new film project as well as two new books. In between I was selling stories to magazines in Japan, New Zealand, and Europe, as well as some of my favorites in the United States. Occasional work in the film industry as a script consultant was also bringing in some nice income when the jobs were offered. Occasional work as a marketing consultant and event promoter continued to further buffer my income.

An editor at *Motorcycle Consumer News* asked if I could prepare a motorcycle for a ride around the world and write a series of articles

about what I had done to make it ready. I agreed, and once finished was challenged by one of my associates to "ride my talk," or ride the prepped Kawasaki KLR650 around the world to prove once more that I could do what I claimed, and that the bike was worthy of a global ride.

The challenge was an interesting one, but I wanted to ride around the world in a way I had not done so before. I also wanted to make it a quick trip, as well as one that would not only keep me in the black but also generate more projects for future trips. I was also committed to staying with one motorcycle without having to dismantle it and ship its myriad parts in an effort to escape high shipping and import costs. I wanted to ride it across all 24 time zones, tagging at least four of the seven continents: North America, Africa, Europe, and Asia. The tough sections would be the shifting yellow sands of the Sahara Desert and the potholed, bombed-out roads through Siberia. I was also committed to leaving video recording equipment behind, lightening my load for photographic equipment only.

The KLR started the world ride from Kawasaki Motors Corporation's, U.S.A. headquarters in Irvine, California. I added aluminum saddlebags to haul my camera equipment and clothes and

This was my work station in the jungle of Panama one hot afternoon. My BMW clutch plate had worn out and I had to replace it. Fortunately, in my spare-parts box I had the foresight to carry a spare clutch plate and the tools needed to make the change. What I wished I had had that afternoon was a BMW mechanic to do the work for me while I watched.

One of the most frustrating and time-consuming parts of the trip through Central America was the border crossings. Bribes and slippery characters seemed to be the best grease to ease the crossings. One problem that I had was the VIN numbers on my motorcycle did not match those on my ownership papers. I had the numbers on the title and registration stamped on two small pieces of metal in a city shopping market at a key shop and glued them onto the motorcycle frame and engine, which solved the problem for the rest of the journey around the world. My cost for the stamped number plates was less than $5.

To get me and my motorcycle from Central America to South America, I wisely chose air flights, saving me numerous days and costing about the same price. Here, the motorcycle is ready to be loaded onto an air cargo flight from Panama City to Bogota, Colombia.

to keep them dry. I strapped saddle panniers, tank panniers, and a tank bag on next, and then installed a taller windscreen to the front fairing pod.

The first leg of the North America crossing was from California to my home in the Big Horn Mountains of Montana. It was a test ride to see how the Kawasaki and I got along.

A mental test of our karma together was a ride up a portion of Arizona Highway 191. This road was formerly posted as Highway 666, the Devil's numbers. Enough people even complained to get the state to change the designation, but road gurus still call it 666. The KLR and I laughed at the Devil, riding north with the desert wind through my hair.

To prepare for the sand tracks of Africa and mud ruts across Siberia, I rode through the Arizona desert and practiced on wet off-roads in Wyoming. The KLR fell down several times, not from mechanical problems but from pilot error. Before riding the rest of the way across North America, I made some minor adjustments to the KLR, such as adding nonslip footpegs and off-road handgrips. A major adjustment was made to the pilot; his right hand had to be throttled back.

Road carnage was common in South America.

Beach camping was my favorite for tent sites. Sometimes I camped in private campgrounds, other times in the wild.

Down the west coast of South America ,the road was dead straight and in very good condition.

The run across the United States to Daytona Bike Week was nearly all on interstate highways at speeds approaching 75 miles per hour. The 650cc engine was strong enough to push the fully loaded motorcycle through the wind to keep up with most of the faster vehicles. It was late February and the temperature was bone-chilling cold until Tennessee. The tank panniers and taller windscreen cut some of the chilled blast from the front. On the flip side, the added comfort was the increased buffeting from trucks and buses. The lightweight KLR was sometimes nearly blown sideways when larger vehicles passed at high speed. I didn't expect this problem anywhere besides the autobahns of Europe.

I could sometimes find roads that ran parallel to the main roadways, often taking me to places where I saw no other tourists or motorcycle travelers.

People often asked where I was headed whenever I stopped for gas or a meal. When I answered "around the world," they would take a longer look at the Kawasaki. Some wanted to know how long it took to circle the globe, and I told them about five months at 4,000 miles per month. Others asked about gas availability and quality. I told them the 5-gallon gas tank could get me at least 150 miles on a full load, and based on my experience from three previous motorcycle rides around the world, I expected to be able to find a gas station in that distance. As for the quality of the gas, I told them the Kawasaki would probably run on any gas I could find, maybe even vodka as I rode across Russia.

While crossing the United States, I was testing not only the KLR and how I had outfitted it, but also myself and my riding gear. An electric liner for my jacket assured me I could keep warm in Siberia. Camping in freezing weather and rain in Kentucky proved that my sleeping bag was warm enough, and I also learned my tent did not leak. I also discovered that I could comfortably sit on the KLR for 8 to 10 hours a day and not feel beat up afterward.

With thousands of cruisers and sport bikes rolling around Daytona Beach during Bike Week, the KLR—prepared for a ride around the world—drew much attention from other motorcyclists. Most observers knew it was a Kawasaki because of the green color. Many wanted to know how I was going to get it across the water to Africa and which route I would take.

Border crossings in South America were much easier and more motorcycle-friendly than in Central America.

The water crossing was accomplished in a shipping container across the Atlantic, while I rode around in Cuba on borrowed motorcycles. The Atlantic crossing took nearly a month by ocean freighter, and although slow, what I saved in shipping costs was what I lived on later.

As for my route, I would point to a map of the world stenciled on the side of one of the aluminum panniers. There, the route was outlined so people would not have to guess at where I meant when speaking of countries such as Latvia or Mauritania.

I was soon in Florida. I drained the gas, took the windshield off, strapped it to the seat, and removed the battery. The KLR and its title were handed over to the shipping agents in Orlando, before being rolled into a container and transported by truck and then boat across the Atlantic. Its next test would be tackling the huge sand dunes of the Sahara Desert.

My goal was to reach Ushuaia, Argentina, by Christmas Day. It was summertime there, and snow was flying around my home north in the United States.

I had a little fun with this roadside stuffed donkey. I did not know why it was there or what it was advertising, but I thought it was colorful enough for a photograph.

Sometime the roads took me into areas that were remote enough that I was the only person or vehicle around.

In the Desert

Berbers, camels, an ocean of sand, and all 40 of Ali Baba's thieves met me when I arrived in Morocco. Africa was the second continent on my 'round-the-world ride with the KLR650. It proved to be a survival challenge for both the motorcycle and myself.

Mamba snakes, lions, hippos, bad roads, a lack of gas, aggressive people with guns, heat, and mechanical breakdowns were things for which I had planned. What I discovered was the KLR performed flawlessly despite the 100-plus-degree temperatures and hammering it across bombed-out roads. The animals left me alone, possibly because I became lean and mean for lack of cold swill at night in the Muslim countries.

Riding in the Sahara Desert had long been a dream, as had been sleeping in my tent listening to the shifting sands of the otherwise quiet nights. Fifty feet into the soft sand turned my dream into a waking nightmare.

The overburdened KLR's front wheel dug deeply into the soft stuff; it didn't fly over the surface like a dirt or Dakar Rally bike. The back wheel spewed clouds of sand 10 feet into the air behind me. If I throttled to a stop in first gear and paddled and pushed on the handlebars, I could manage 20 feet in a minute. At that speed my ride across the Sahara would have taken me from dead tired to old age before a lion could have found and eaten me.

After a day of flogging and flopping in the 120-degree sand, I realized why most overland motorcycle riders of the Sahara loaded their luggage onto trucks and rode behind them when crossing the soft stuff. Some motorcyclists pitched their motorcycle onto the truck too, but most did not write about that. I decided my KLR and I were meant to ride, so I turned around and headed back to firm ground, discarding my dream and the haunting Sahara adventure.

A band of Berbers offered to let me sleep in their tents for the night. They had heard my motorcycle coming through the dunes and sent a boy out to see what all the noise and screaming of obscenities was about. He guided me to their compound where I was offered tea, palm dates, and a meal of goat soup. After the meal they passed around some evil smelling desert brew, and my motorcycle and I became the subject of the jabbering and hand waving. No one spoke English, I understood no Berber, but we managed some back and forth with our French and sign language.

I declined the alcohol and paid for my meal with some Kawasaki stickers I carried as calling cards. After an hour, some of my hosts became surly from the swill. Visions of me in a stewpot or robbed, bikeless and naked, caused me to make up a story about needing to meet a friend. I rode off into the Saharan sunset and found a camping spot well away from my new drumbeating friends, some of whom had Kawasaki stickers stuck on their foreheads when I left.

Camels were a problem. They caused me to crash at speed. I was riding on a high-speed gravel road, enjoying the wide-open land. As I topped a small hill, a herd of dromedaries that had been lying in the jeep tracks just over the rise stood up. Rather than plow through them, I veered to the right and into a ditch of soft sand. The motorcycle slowed faster than I did. I flew over the handlebars and tried to bury my helmeted head in the ditch sand like an ostrich. The show for the camels must have been their most interesting event in weeks, but they did not move. They stood by peacefully, looking at the toppled motorcycle and me.

Nothing on the motorcycle was broken except my wounded pride, but not from the crash itself. As I struggled for half an hour in the heat, the beasts of burden watched me from their pleasant repose in the sand, and I envied their nonchalant way with the world. With nothing to throw at them other than handfuls of sand and verbal abuses, I imagined their bemusement of this rider in the sand on the side of their road. As I rode off, I noticed they had settled back down to enjoy their mid-day chew and snooze.

Theft plagued me. Anything that was removable from the motorcycle disappeared. Pens stuck in the sides of my tank bag would go missing after a gas stop. Bungee cords would spring off seemingly on their own when I stopped and shopped at a market. Anytime I would park, I put the bike cover over the motorcycle to keep prying eyes and hands off, at least until Ali Baba or one of his workers stole the cover.

When I asked a local Moroccan why pilfering things off my motorcycle was so popular, he answered, "It's like the national sport here. The boys like to show off to their friends what they were able to steal from the Western traveler. Consider it their merit badges if they were a Boy Scout."

After hunting for the Marrakesh Express made famous by Crosby, Stills, and Nash in 1969, I sadly discovered there was no express train to Marrakesh. Next I rode to Casablanca in hopes of finding Rick's American Cafe, imagining Humphrey Bogart saying "Play it again, Sam." Again my search came up dry, like trying to find snow in a desert.

I knew snow was on top of Mount Kilimanjaro, the world's highest free-standing mountain at 19,340 feet. It was far to the south, however, and as I had failed to ride across the Sahara, it was nearly impossible to reach Kilimanjaro due to borders being closed to American tourists

These mountains in southern Argentina reminded me of the Rocky Mountains of North America.

like myself. In the north, I had little hope of getting out of the heat and into the white stuff. Then an Algerian told me, "Yes, yes, we have snow. Go to the Atlas Mountains." There I found a ski slope and lodge, but no snow in May. It was close enough, though, for adventuring in Africa, and I considered my journey to the dark continent successful.

The KLR never missed a beat as it thumped through the toughest riding conditions Africa could throw at it. However, the clock was ticking on my 'round-the-world ride as the Swiss Alps loomed far to the north: they were my European target. The high-speed autobahns crossing Europe would also be a challenge for the 650cc single.

Screaming monkeys was what I found after leaving Africa. Winston Churchill said that as long as there were monkeys on the 2.3-square-mile Rock of Gibraltar at the southern tip of Spain, the colony would be British. I booked the KLR and myself on a ferryboat across the Mediterranean Sea and left the African continent to land in Spain, my first country as I started across the European continent. I first wanted to see if the monkeys were still on Gibraltar.

To verify the existence of monkeys, I had to wait for commercial airplanes to land before riding across the runway of the airport that separates Gibraltar from Spain, the only road into the colony. While waiting for a plane to touch down, my Kawasaki was closely inspected by Spanish customs officials and other waiting motorcyclists. The American version of the KLR650 was not imported into Europe, so it was unique enough to merit their attention, especially outfitted the way it was.

Once I got to the top of the Rock of Gibraltar, I determined it still should be British. The English monkeys were far from friendly. They tried to steal anything on my motorcycle they could, such as my mirrors or maps in the tank bag, even the sunglasses I was wearing inside my helmet and my camera as I tried to take a picture. They shrieked, hissed, and howled when I beat them off. I left the thieving and screaming primates to the British on the Rock and began crossing my third continent.

Europe has one of the best highway systems on the planet. If I wanted to cross a country quickly, I could pay the fees for using the newer, multilane, warp-speed highways. Some were free, others were expensive, but they all had the same rule: the left lane was for passing only, for the big dogs. Imagine riding at 90 miles per hour and being passed by some red Italian or gray German car traveling at 150 miles per hour or better. The downside to the autobahns was high speed meant high consumption of gas. At nearly $6 a gallon, it would cost me $30 or more to fill my tank if I wanted to run at the higher speeds, covering only two-thirds the distance I could at slower cruising speeds.

A broken BMW about as far from a BMW repair shop made me a new friend. He needed a new clutch plate and someone who knew how to take the old one out and put the new one in. I surprised him when I told him I was carrying what he needed and that I was a certified BMW mechanic.

Europe, with the formation of the European Union, had become expensive. Where Spain and France used to be bargains, I was looking at EU prices of $150 to $200 per day while on the road. A side trip to the Alps of Switzerland cost $25 for a basic plate of spaghetti and $5 for a soda. A simple sleeping room in a quiet village was close to $100. At those prices I decided to ride through as quickly as possible to limit my credit card's exposure to the new European Union.

Asia was my next destination, straight across Russia's eight time zones. There were no Kawasaki dealers, no easily acquired tires, and surely no roadside-assistance plan. I would be flying without a safety net. I decided to make a pit stop in Germany at an authorized Kawasaki dealer in Heidelberg. The KLR was due to have the valve clearances checked, its oil and filters changed, and its tires replaced.

It was a quick pit stop. Engine clearances were found to be well within specifications, even after hammering the high-speed highways of North America and Europe and flogging the blazing hot sands of Africa. No mechanical adjustments were needed. The chain didn't even have to be adjusted, and the sprockets were holding up fine.

My route across Europe took me northeast through Spain, France, Switzerland, Austria, Germany, Czechoslovakia, Poland, Lithuania, and finally to Latvia. Except for Poland, the roads were in superb condition, allowing me to travel in the 60-mile-per-hour range, where I was getting the best mileage per gallon while still staying with traffic.

Gas was easy to find. Many stations surpassed the amenities that I was used to in the United States. Nearly all took credit cards, and some offered some high-test juice at the 98-octane level, which my

Camping in the national park south of Ushuaia found me as far south as I could ride on the South American continent on Christmas Day, 1997.

KLR may have liked but did not need. In one gas station I found not only the usual mini-mart and clean restrooms, but also a bank of computer terminals that took coins or credit cards to connect with the Internet.

Whenever I stopped, whether at a restaurant or guesthouse for the night, my Kawasaki drew attention. Not only were many of the Europeans motorcycle-friendly, having owned motorcycles themselves, they could see I was on a long journey by the way the KLR was outfitted.

My limited German, Spanish, and French usually got me into a language zone of English and a mix of the others. Many people were impressed that I was on a long ride around the globe, but my American citizenship prompted the most questions. Several invited me home for a meal and free place to stay, while others helped me with directions and suggestions for sleeping, eating, and problem avoidance in their respective countries. In a heavy rain storm in Spain, one man told me to wait under a covered store front while he went home, got his own motorcycle, and then escorted me through town to make sure I did not get lost. He insisted on buying me a cup of hot coffee and toasted sandwich at a local restaurant, and then gave me his telephone number to call if I had any problems.

Some nights I camped to save money. The European campgrounds were private and well maintained. Almost all had a restaurant, laundry, and small store selling everything from noodles to beer. Some offered swimming pools and spas. An interesting tenting option in many campgrounds was the small, enclosed travel trailers called caravans. These had electricity, cold running water, and sometimes gas ovens, but no toilets. They were dry and one-third the price of an inexpensive room in a nearby guesthouse or pension. I would camp in

I marked my spot at kilometer marker 2080 by building a rock formation.

The rock structure looked solid enough to withstand the winds on Patagonia. Sometime later I was told by other travelers it had been torn down. On a second trip to Ushuaia, I built a larger replacement. Again it was removed or demolished. The mystery of its disappearance is one of the secrets blowing in the winds of Patagonia.

a trailer when it was raining or cold, my sleeping bag serving as the bed sheets and my riding jacket liner as my pillow. The motorcycle would be safely parked just outside the door versus in a hotel parking lot out of my sight, unattended.

My travel time across the European continent was less than a month. I spent some time in Germany visiting friends who insisted on putting together a going away party for me, knowing I was headed across the bleak Russian tundra. I stopped to tour two motorcycle museums in Germany and spent three days riding my favorite roads in the Alps, but I was on a tight schedule. I had prepaid for a low-cost flight back to the United States from a far eastern port of Russia, and it was going to be expensive if I had to change the flight or purchase another ticket.

Iguazu Falls in Brazil merited a stop long enough to take this photograph.

After leaving Latvia and crossing the border into Russia, I had a month and eight times zones to negotiate before reaching the Sea of Japan, my next rest stop, with the huge, unknown expanse of Siberia in between.

The road into Moscow was well paved and made for an easy one-day ride. Gas stations were modern and plentiful. It was on this section that I met a Belgian motorcyclist and his sister who claimed to have ridden in Russia eight times. When he learned of the proposed route from Moscow across Siberia, he said I was taking the "Road to Hell" and implied I would likely die. While I knew there were no Kawasaki dealers along that section—and in some places no bridges— the thought of death from crashing on a bad road had not been part of my plan. The fact that there was only one road across Russia did not leave me much choice or time to worry about other options. I discounted the Belgium's trepidation, knowing that he had probably never seen a gravel road in Belgium and noting his dirt-free motorcycle and riding gear.

In Moscow, the Kawasaki was a crowd collector. The Russians had not seen a KLR650, as it was not imported to Russia, nor one as outfitted as mine for serious overland travel. My KLR said

I stayed in Rio de Janeiro only long enough to take this photo. The millions of people and heat were oppressive to me after having been alone and away from the masses for so long. I did not spend more than 15 minutes on the beach.

My host in Brazil could not tolerate my BMW being so dirty after the thousands of miles it had traveled, so he gave it its first bath in three months.

"Independent Traveler," a foreign concept for many Russians. They were even more surprised to learn I was an American setting out to cross Siberia, alone. The KLR and my solo adventure made me many friends in Moscow. In Red Square, a Russian couple blessed my Kawasaki with a Christian prayer and insisted I carry a small gold Saint Christopher charm they gave me, Saint Christopher being, of course, the patron saint of travelers.

One error I made before entering Russia was not purchasing a good Russian road map. I had been promised the use of a GPS, but that promise fell through when the owner took it with him when he returned to Germany. I did have a three-page fold-out map of the world I had ripped out of an airline magazine, and I thought I would find a map at a gas station along the way. What I learned crossing Siberia was Russian gas stations sell gas, not maps, and little else.

Other than how to say "hello," "thank you," and "toilet," my Russian was limited to what I learned along the way, such as how to pronounce the name of the next major town. Sometimes I could communicate in broken English or German, but found hand signs and finger pointing worked as well.

Eating was a daily challenge. The restaurant menus were all in Russian, so usually I would point at something and eat what was

I hit this snake in Brazil. I hate snakes and stopped only long enough to make sure it was dead. Although I spoke no Portuguese, I could understand that the villagers were congratulating me on my successful kill as they invited me to share dinner with them with the snake in the stew pot. I passed on the invitation.

brought. For breakfast and lunch, I usually purchased meals at small stores or open-air public markets. I usually took dinner in a café or restaurant for my main meal of the day. Whatever food I was brought I would wash down with vodka, the national drink, which seemed to be more popular than water.

The last fast food I saw was a McDonald's in Moscow. Popular along my route were restaurants converted from old railroad cars. While I could not read the signs on the outside, I learned that if it looked like a modified railroad car it was probably a café.

Sleeping was a bit trickier on my limited budget. Overpriced government-operated tourist hotels were seldom marked and often off the main road through towns. Smaller hotels were alongside the main highway but many times unmarked. Sometimes I would see trucks parked around a building and could find a sleeping room inside, a

I crossed the equator again, this time going from south to north. I would cross it two more times on this trip around the world.

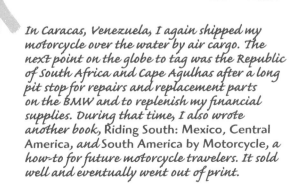

Almost daily rains sometimes made roads so slippery that it was better to wait overnight for the roads to dry out and drive as much as possible the next morning until afternoon rains began again.

In Caracas, Venezuela, I again shipped my motorcycle over the water by air cargo. The next point on the globe to tag was the Republic of South Africa and Cape Agulhas after a long pit stop for repairs and replacement parts on the BMW and to replenish my financial supplies. During that time, I also wrote another book, Riding South: Mexico, Central America, and South America by Motorcycle, a how-to for future motorcycle travelers. It sold well and eventually went out of print.

Everywhere I stopped, people wanted to look at or touch my motorcycle. Several times I gave kids a ride only to discover more were popping out of the village to take advantage of my generosity.

In Botswana I was able to ride alongside and through herds of elephants.

simple bed with shared bathroom at the end of the hall. Once, in a rainstorm, the manager of one of the truck stops took pity on me. She woke a sleeping truck driver, introduced me to him (Ivan), and told him I was going to sleep in the other bed in his room. Sleepily he said one word—"*Da,*"—which means "yes," and crawled back under his blankets. As quietly as I could, I got out of my wet riding gear and went to sleep under the gift of dry bedding.

Ivan and I sawed logs through the night. Somewhere around 5 a.m., he dressed and slipped out of our room. Later that day I passed him driving his truck, and his flashing headlights and wildly honking horn told me I had made a new friend when I stopped.

I used my tent and sleeping bag three to five times a week. While there were no campgrounds, I found small roads leading off into wooded areas for seclusion. A cold dinner of bread, wurst, and soda would suffice instead of a hotel restaurant meal, and the savings I spent on indoor sleeping and eating the next night.

Gasoline was plentiful, though the octane level was never high. The Kawasaki KLR650 thumped along well with any gasoline poured in the tank, even the 80-octane level stuff. I thought that if I did need some petrol boost I could add a pint of vodka, which was also plentiful.

There were many wide-open spaces in Africa that seemed empty until I stopped, and then magically people would appear. There is a saying, "You're never alone in Africa." It was seemingly true, especially when I would camp or stop to take photographs.

A bad road through Zambia was reflective of how poor the country was.

I was faced with a major decision in Chita. I could put the KLR on a train and ride for three days over a 900-mile section called the Zilof Gap. The other option was to ride the incomplete section of road and chance not finding trucks to carry the motorcycle through the numerous streams that had no bridges and were too deep and swift to cross. The ticking toward my expiring visa and recent heavy rains found me opting for riding the rails. Unfortunately, all the seats and baggage out of Chita on passenger trains were booked for several weeks ahead, as I was in the high-summer season for travelers. With my limited Russian and the help of some local motorcycle acquaintances, we found another way: pay cash behind the back of a shipping office and ride in a cargo car of a train.

Each cargo car had two employees who rode in it, overseeing loading and unloading along the route. I paid the cash to the two men

This type of road tested my off-pavement riding skills, sometimes for hours on end.

My BMW did not like this type of sand at any speed. Lowering tire pressure only meant I would have to inflate it back up later and seemed not to improve handling at the speeds I was able to maintain.

in my car and slipped more money to a train station man to look the other way while my motorcycle and I were secretly hoisted aboard when station officials were on a vodka break. Inside, I tied the motorcycle down, erected my tent behind some crates not visible from the door, and spent the next three nights camping in the cargo car. When the train stopped at a town, I was told to hide and stay out of sight from the police and railroad officials since I had no ticket or cargo manifest. I was instructed to give some money to the cargo men at these stops, and they would go to the local store or food shop and buy me sandwiches, water, or soft drinks.

Each cargo car was equipped with a grungy toilet and shower and a hot plate for warming food. My cargo car was the most popular in the 30- to 40-car train because my two cargo men operated the unofficial vodka concession. At each stop we had many visitors from

Victoria Falls
merited a stop.

While passing through
Zimbabwe, I found the country's
turmoil had created a shortage
of gasoline. Several times I spent
hours trying to find and purchase
gas from venders who sold it out
of soda bottles.

other cargo cars, all who soon knew an illegal motorcycle traveler was inside and wanted to meet me and look at the Kawasaki. I was invited to other cargo cars several times for meals between stops. With my limited Russian and their even more limited English, we managed to become friendly over the endless Russian swill. Looking back on the entire ride across Russia, I have the fondest memories from that train ride. Not only was it fun, but it saved me more than a week of travel time through some very boring parts of Siberia, and it only cost me a quarter of what it would have cost had I paid for gas and truck rides on the other route choice.

When I unloaded the motorcycle in Khabarovsk, members of a local motorcycle club met me. They had been contacted by my new motorcycle friends in Chita and knew I was coming and when. They took me to their clubhouse, introduced me to their club members, and

Somewhere in Africa, I saw it posted that this was the biggest tree on the continent. I don't know if it was true or just an advertising ploy, but it hooked me.

I tried some sand riding after unloading all of my luggage and emptying my aluminum panniers. The BMW seemed to slow and sink into the sand just as fast with the lightened load.

While I did not carry a portable computer, I was able to find inexpensive Internet cafés throughout Africa, enabling me to check mail from my businesses and friends about once a week.

Africa means animals. It was rare to find this one alongside the road outside of a protected game park, and the giraffe was as interested in me as I was in it. Most of the wild game outside safaris or national parks had been decimated over the years by the local population looking for food.

This monkey and his friends visited my campsite one afternoon. Later, after dark, they attacked my motorcycle, tearing into the tank bag and side panniers. They broke one of my gas cables, a spare part I did not carry. I had to drive on one cylinder the next morning to the nearest town to find a replacement cable.

asked me to sign their world traveler map on the wall. My Kawasaki KLR was the first they had seen and was a major point of interest for the evening party they put on for me. They were impressed that the Kawasaki had never missed a beat, had a flat tire, or needed any maintenance across the entire length of Russia. Several offered to buy it, but I told them I still had a long ride ahead to complete my ride around the world before I would consider selling it.

I rode the next two days into Vladivostok, wondering how I could get the motorcycle crated and on a flight to Los Angeles. There I hoped to collect it and ride to Mexico. With four days left on my visa, I managed to find one air freight company that would take the motorcycle (crated, drained of fuel, and battery removed), if only I could get it into a box small enough to fit into the side door of their plane. A flurry of paperwork with customs officials, a handful of U.S. dollars to a freight company that used a pizza restaurant's telephone number, and

I tried riding a camel. I did not like it and it did not like me. This one refused to stand, and when its handler tried to make it do so, it turned its head back far enough to try to bite me. Another one spit on me. I don't think I make a good camel rider.

This was a rare photograph. I found the cheetah alongside a fence to an animal park. I suspected it had gotten through the fence and was trying to find a way back in where it knew there was daily food.

promises by Russian mafia businessmen saw my motorcycle sealed in the customs house with a promise it would be in Los Angeles two days later.

Flying into Los Angeles, I wasn't worried about the scratches on the Kawasaki, clearing the motorcycle through U.S. customs, how I was going to put it back together by myself, or how I would even get it out of the airport without any gas and possibly a dead battery from being in an upside-down crate. My lingering worries were about the wad of cash I had handed over to the vodka-drinking shipping agent who kept waving his hand to signify "Don't worry!" whenever I pointed at the date on the calendar when the motorcycle was promised to be in Los Angeles. Sure enough, my worries were warranted when the motorcycle failed to arrive even a week after the promised date.

Russian blackmail was "Don't worry" translated. After nearly three weeks of frustration, e-mailing, telephone calls, and letters to the U.S. embassy in Moscow, the Russian air cargo company in Vladivostok finally flew the promised KLR to Los Angeles. What eventually broke the crated box loose from the grips of the Russian businessmen were additional funds wired to an unnamed international numbered bank account, funds well above the initially agreed-upon cash payment. The Russian air cargo company called it "doing business." I called it "getting screwed." For a professional motorcycle adventurer, I was kicking myself for having been exploited as easily as some greenhorn foreign traveler.

Once the KLR arrived in Los Angeles, it was quickly cleared through customs and deposited on the tarmac outside the air cargo

This was an ugly section of road that made me long for the wide, paved freeways of America and Europe.

I affixed one of my personal stickers to the door of this campground. Five or six years later, I received an e-mail from a fellow motorbike traveler who had stopped at the same campground and saw my sticker, proving how small the world has become with the Internet.

This was my destination for Africa, Cape Agulhas. I had tagged another touch point on my ride around the world.

On the way north through Europe, I spotted these two BMWs. Neither was real, but I lusted after both after I had been beating up my slow and tired R80G/S.

I had been to Europe many times before, so I made a speedy trip north from Stuttgart to the North Cape. It took three nights, and I spent little time as a tourist. Here, I was passing through Sweden on a windy day. I stopped long enough for gas, food, and to take a few photographs.

I once again crossed the Arctic Circle, though the last time was a world away in Alaska.

company's loading dock. With no petrol in the gas tank, no battery, and no lifts to get the wheels back on, I spent an afternoon reassembling the motorcycle and discarding the crate. Back in one piece, I inserted the key, switched on the ignition, and the Kawasaki jumped back to life.

An hour later it was parked at Kawasaki Motors Corporation, U.S.A. headquarters in Irvine for a quick photo shoot. Technically, it was back at its original starting point, but I wanted to make sure all my 'round-the-world dots were connected, so I started looking at the map, realizing my true second start point was in Colorado where the initial challenge had originated.

Ugly weather in the Rocky Mountains had me looking south instead of north for the return to my start point at Denver, Colorado. Route 2 across the top of Mexico would get the KLR into warmer weather, off the interstates, and into another country. It would also give it another 1,000 miles, on and off the road.

The many stamps in my passport and entry and exit documents attached to the Kawasaki title and registration eased crossing the border into Mexico. One Mexican customs official thumbed through my passport, saw the entry stamp for Spain, and asked in Spanish how I had liked it. I told him Spain was great, except for the new high prices since Spain had joined the European Union. He laughed

While cars and trucks were charged a fee on this roadway, motorcycles were allowed to travel for free.

One of the nice things about traveling through Europe was the ease of which my motorcycle and I could cross borders. Not once in Europe was I ever asked to produce paperwork other than the time I got a speeding ticket. An exception was made when I drove onto one of several ferry boats to cross water. There I was asked to show ownership papers and proof of insurance.

One of the wonders of my global travel had been seeing American Indian teepees as far away from America as they could possibly be, like finding a motorcycle stuck in the snow at the South Pole. While I knew a Japanese fellow had once ridden a motorcycle to the South Pole, I was also aware that he did not leave it there. In this lonely spot above the Arctic Circle in Europe, I suspected there had been few American Indians, and those who were there were only passing through.

My fishing hobby found me stopping when I saw this fisherman with a bucketful of fish. While we had a language barrier, he understood I wanted to try my luck fishing by using his boat and some rented or borrowed fishing tackle. He was a fine man and offered me several of the fish he had netted out of his catch for free.

and said, "You will feel the same here in Mexico. Since we joined the North American Free Trade Agreement all our prices have gone up."

The KLR was still performing flawlessly. At every stop, whether for gas, food, or sleeping, local people would look at the motorcycle and ask either where I was going or where I had been. I would point to the map of the world on the side of my aluminum saddlebag while trying to answer in broken Spanish. The most perplexing question was if my start was in Denver and I had landed in Los Angeles, why was I in Mexico? The best answer I could muster was, "I like the food." That was easier than telling the truth: that since both my Kawasaki and I were running well and I had some money and time left, I wanted to stay on the road rather than end the ride of a lifetime.

I crossed the border back into the United States and changed my watch to Mountain Standard time. I realized when I did I had

To reach the North Cape, I had to use several ferry boats to cross bodies of water. They were reasonably priced and part of the roadway system.

I reached the North Cape on a cold and windy day. I was not allowed to take my motorcycle out of the parking lot for a picture at the North Cape sign, so had to play tourist until the facility closed.

The North Cape was as far north on the European continent as I could reach by motorcycle; I had tagged another touch point in the planned ride around the world.

For the third ride around the world, I crossed the United States and the North American continent using my 1947 Indian Chief. As much as I love the old marchine, I tired of having to make repairs almost daily, tightening loose nuts and bolts and seeing to other, more problematic repairs.

To cross the South American continent, I used an Amazonas motorcycle. There were only about 350 of these manufactured, five with matching sidecars. The motorcycle, when made, was the world's largest motorcycle and used a Volkswagen engine and transmission, which included a reverse gear. The police in Brazil favored the Amazonas because at slow speeds, such as in parades and doing escort work, they would not heat up like the air-cooled Harley-Davidsons. The Amazonas kept the huge motor cooling fan in front.

then crossed all 24 time zones. It was celebration time. To mark the occasion, I spent a quiet night camping in the desert, reflecting on the ride around the world. As I rode across a stretch of desert, I forgot to focus on the sand in front of me instead of the mountains on the horizon. At the last possible second, I saw the only rock in the desert, one the size of a football. "Shit!" I yelled, clamping the front brake lever to the handlebar and flying over the windshield when the KLR landed after hopping the rock. Again, only my ego was bruised. I had managed to avoid serious injury to myself and the Kawasaki for nearly 30,000 miles only to make a possible serious error one day away from my beginning point. You know what they say: most auto accidents occur close to home. But it was a wakeup call; I wasn't finished with my long ride yet.

Back in Denver, where I started my journey five months earlier, I parked the KLR and spent the next weeks catching up on life away

I met members of the Amazonas Motorcycle Club in Brazil. They wondered why an American would be riding in their part of the world on a Brazilian-made marchine versus an American-made Harley-Davidson. Since I spoke almost no Portuguese and none of them spoke much English, I still doubt they understood why I wanted to use a motorcycle made on the continent I was tagging. It made no difference at the time; they were a fun group.

from my office. Bills and taxes had to be paid, parents visited, friends contacted, and contractual obligations met. My daily life of the KLR and me, together, on the road around the globe, started to drift to gray from the colors of places such as the golden Sahara sands of Morocco, Lenin's Red Square, and yellow sunflowers of June in Germany.

The KLR languished in my garage. It needed an oil change and a good once-over to check what may or may not have held up during our long trip together. I noted that it had not consumed any coolant nor brake fluid. The chain and sprockets showed some wear, but I was surprised how little. Valve clearances were still within specifications, and the spark plug looked ready for another 10,000 miles. I replaced the rear tire and changed the front tire and both tubes. After a day's work and a good cleaning, the KLR looked and rode like it was ready for another long ride.

The KLR ride around the world covered 19,631 ground miles and took five months. I had crossed all 24 times zones, and other than the one small get-off in Mexico, I had a relatively smooth ride. Two flat tires were the only mechanical problems encountered.

In May 2010 I donated the 'round-the-world KLR650 to the National Motorcycle Museum. While it had nearly 40,000 miles on the odometer at the time, I felt it still had another global tour left in it.

One of my adventure-riding friends was fascinated with my trip and wanted to take a long solo trip too. He was unwilling to call himself an adventurer, however, to which I agreed up to a point. We debated whether one had to ride around the world to become an adventurer or merely make a ride to the supermarket. I shared with him some of my thoughts: "Adventure gardening" was how the road sign described the

I used a BMW to cross the European continent.

The BMW was perfect for the high-speed roadways across Europe. The only drawback was having to return it to its home base in Germany after I had gone as far east as I could.

I flew into Delhi, India, and outfitted this new Enfield 500 Bullet to use as far east as I could go.

farm shop in Montana. "Adventure reading" was o   over of a book about a canoe trip. "Adventure Hotel" was the name of a motel. "Adventure riding" was used to promote a high-end motorcycle tour of the Alps.

I wondered where the risk was in growing vegetables. Maybe it was losing the crop of tomatoes to bugs or birds, or not being able to eat organically grown food from your garden. As for adventure reading of a book, I do most of my book reading on my back in bed. Maybe the risk was I would fall asleep and the book would tumble from my fingers. As for the adventure hotel, I could imagine, given

I only let these monks sit on the motorcycle and have their picture taken after learning my lesson about giving children short rides on my motorcycle in Africa. One monk wanted to try on my motorcycle helmet and I let him. Three days later, I had the same head lice he'd had. I had learned another lesson—keep your helmet to yourself.

the right company, oils, latex products, ropes, restraints, electrical aids, and furniture, there could be the risk of death from a heart attack or asphyxiation.

Adventure riding in the Alps? That one perplexed me. The tour company offered local riding guides in the front and back of the group with catered lunch stops, four- and five-star hotels, luggage handling, an onboard mechanic in the chase van that carried tools, spare parts, and a retractable awning to provide shade or shelter in case of rain. Adventure motorcycle riding was a conundrum, and given the pictures in the brochure, an oxymoron at best. The advertisement seemed to promote the fact that all risk had been removed from the motorcycle tour. If the motorcycle had a flat tire or quit running, the mechanic would hop out and make the repairs while the motorcyclist sat in a chair under the awning sipping a cold soda or bottle of mineral water while posting pictures and words on the Internet.

I parked the Enfield near the Chinese border in Sikkim and tried riding a yak.

I tried a Hartford motorcycle to cross Taiwan. I was still in Asia and used a Taiwanese Hartford for this leg of the world tour.

I finished Taiwan on an SYM motorcycle like most of the locals used as daily commuters. The limitations, besides the limited luggage space, was they were not allowed on the super highways.

I learned the small SYM was not allowed on the super highways when I was stopped by a traffic policeman. There was no chance to outrun him on his BMW. He was nice enough to escort me off the super highway and not give me a ticket in exchange for one of my personalized stickers.

One night I was sharing my perplexities of the definition of adventure riding with a female motorcyclist when she hammered me with a bold statement: "You're no adventure rider; your business card states you are a 'Professional Motorcycle Adventurer.'"

Shamed, I knew she was right. Twenty-five years ago, when I designed the business card and letterhead, defining what I thought to be my profession, Robert Hellman, the late editor of the *BMW on the Level* magazine, pinned me like a butterfly on display when he challenged my title. I thought then I had a solid understanding of the word *adventure*, what a motorcycle was, and where the line was drawn between the amateur and the professional. Ordinarily I would bristle as a relative newbie to remote off-pavement motorcycling called me out, as my dinner guest had done. However, I had been with her

Here is my personal sticker that I have given away or pasted up around the world. I found them to be better than business cards. Somewhere on the planet there are between 5,000 and 10,000 of them.

I finished my third ride around the globe using this 2001 Harley-Davidson. I learned it did not like sand but loved the paved roadways. Of all the motorcycles I had used, this one had the best radio. It also was the only motorcycle I used that ever even had a radio.

In 2002, I used a 2001 Kawasaki KLR650 for my fourth ride around the world. This was a poster prepared by Kawasaki after I had completed the world ride.

113

I discovered that I could crash as easily in Taiwan as I could on other continents around the globe.

I earned this sticker after being told I was not an adventure rider, rather an avid rider.

jungle riding on a lonely dirt track in Thailand near the Burmese border when we had come upon a group of military men who flagged us down. She handled herself well. I also knew her to own a pretty solid stable of motorcycles, including two V-Stroms, one '08 KLR650, a ST1100, and a well-worn Honda Silverwing.

"So if I am not a motorcycle adventurer who has made a profession of it, what am I?"

She asked how many miles I logged each year, and I replied, "Maybe 40 to 50,000, depending on my money and time."

"Didn't you get called a 'Total Fanatic' by one well-known motor-journalist for your lone-wolf lifestyle, commitment, and dedication to motorcycles, motorcycle racing, motorcycle repairing, and your work in the industry as a motorcycle magazine journalist and author?"

"Yes, well, I was in some pretty heavy company when I got dubbed with that. There were four others who were at the top of that list with me, so the fanaticism was spread around between us."

"Do you choose motorcycle wrenching and journeying over Twitter and posting on Facebook, or do you even bother with a blog?"

Hanging my head, I had to admit not doing any of the three, let alone when given an option to two-wheel motorized pursuits.

"Well then, you're an avid motorcyclist."

She opened her purse and handed me a sticker, saying, "Put this on your motorcycle or helmet. It says you are way out there, in a category that is clearly defined. You are not an adventure poseur over your keyboard. You, and the others who have this sticker, are avid riders."

"Ok, I'll sticker my helmet or panniers with your sticker if you'll paste my sticker on your motorcycle."

One of my 'round-the-world travel friends once told me that the sign of a true professional motorcyclist is to display they have no ego and take the time to photograph and publish their mistakes. Here was mine after having nearly circled the globe, taking my eyes off the ground in front of me and hitting the only rock around for miles.

I donated this Kawasaki KLR650 to the National Motorcycle Museum after completing another 'round-the-world ride.

Here's my stock 2001 Kawasaki KLR650 before prepping it for a series of articles for a motorcycle magazine on what it would take to make the KLR650 ready for a 'round-the-world ride.

From the start point in Irvine, California, I rode across the United States through Arizona, where I tested some equipment, and then to a second start in Denver, where I made more minor changes and then headed to Florida.

In Florida, I placed the KLR650 in a shipping container for a slow float across the Atlantic while I wandered around Cuba for a few weeks.

I gave her one of my stickers. It reads "Motorcycle Sexpedition—Absolute Riding." I explained that I had been doing field research on the topic by using volunteer consultants who were motorcycle enthusiasts riding to distant places on the globe. By badging her motorcycle or helmet, she would become one of the research assistants.

Pocketing my sticker, she blushed when she said, "That is the kind of adventure riding I can relate to, but before becoming part of your wild, licentious team of researchers, I think I had better ask my boyfriend."

I pulled out another sticker and said, "Give this one to him. I could use a real avid rider team on the project."

Rules of the Road

In my travels around the world, I'd learned a few things:

- Nothing I had done had not been done before by someone else. Motorcyclists had been circling the earth with motorcycles for nearly 100 years.
- Other round-the-world riders had ridden more miles while circling the globe, stayed on the road longer, used larger and smaller motorcycles to complete their trips, had spent more or less money than I, and had done it faster and with more flair and color. What made my rides different was I had done them my way; they were my personal achievements, pushing my personal driving envelope as well as my defined search for adventure.
- Every globe-riding motorcyclist had his or her own adventure envelope to push in the journey.

My destination was Africa and the sands of Sahara.

Heading north from Africa, I stopped in Gibraltar long enough to see if monkeys were still on the rock in the background, which would mean Gibraltar was still British, according to Winston Churchill. The monkeys were there, and they were mean, nasty, and really, really ugly. I concluded the British could keep them and the rock.

Moving through Europe found me camping to save money versus paying for expensive nights sleeping indoors.

117

Red Square in Moscow was as a bustling place.

9   400   9A   10   10A

The best part of my ride across Siberia, where I had the most fun, was riding in a cargo car on a cargo freight train. Siberia itself was pretty boring: mile after mile of scrub brush. My three days and nights camped in the cargo car were spent making new friends, learning how to drink vodka with the train workers, and sneaking in and out of the cargo car while it was moving because I had paid "black money" to the workers to ride the train. Here, I and my motorcycle are sneaking into the cargo car in Chita after having paid the officials to take a break and look the other way.

When the KLR650 finally arrived in the United States from Russia, I had to reassemble it, find gas, and dispose of the shipping crate. It had been held hostage by nefarious "businessmen" in Russia until I wired additional funds to some numbered account to secure its release— my introduction to how business was conducted and cash profits were made.

- If unsure about the availability of gasoline up ahead, fill up.
- I was happier traveling alone than with others. Alone, a journey becomes a personal quest, *my* journey or *my* adventure, not *our* journey or shared adventure. I did not like following a motorcycle in front of me, nor having to worry about one (or more) behind me. I prefer to go it alone.
- I was far less patient than I had thought.
- Death on the roads of the globe did not scare me. What scared me was being in an accident and ending up in some hospital bed unable to move or speak, with the person who had caused the accident in the bed next to me.
- While some travelers claimed it was the journey, for me it had become how long I could keep going on journeys and how many miles I would eventually cover.
- I still was afraid of any adventure that involved snakes or sharks.
- Motorcycles were merely machines or tools, not having a human-like personality. I had never given one a name, although I had had referred to several as a bitch or son-of-a-bitch or bastard after they broke or tossed me off.
- Never take a motorcycle I could not financially afford to lose due to fire, theft, damage, or confiscation into any third-world country.
- Fishing was a fun hobby, but motorcycling had accelerated past a hobby and into a profession.

Back at my start point in Denver, Colorado, the KLR650 was photographed with two of my motorcycles used on other 'round-the-world rides: a 1981 BMW R80G/S and a 1947 Indian Chief. The BMW and Kawasaki eventually were donated to motorcycle museums.

CHAPTER SEVEN

TAKING IT TO EXTREMES

Touring the Most Isolated Spots on the Earth

As I had been circling the globe, I met numerous other motorcycle travelers who were either doing the same thing I was or had in one way or another done the same. It seemed to me there was not much in the way of circumnavigating the globe that had not been done before.

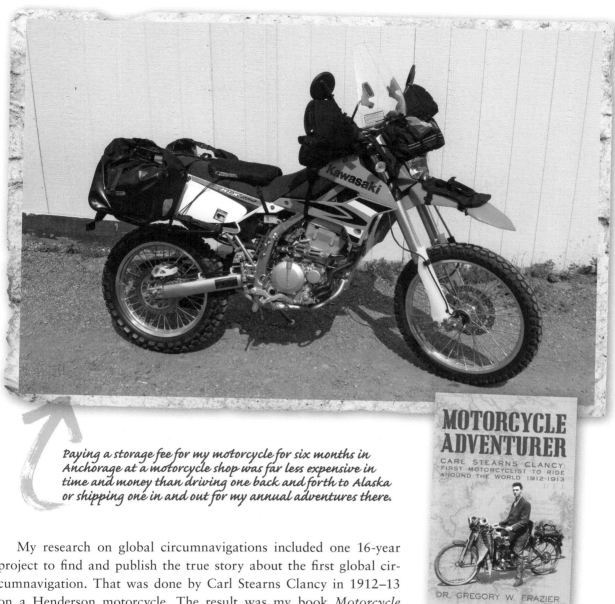

Paying a storage fee for my motorcycle for six months in Anchorage at a motorcycle shop was far less expensive in time and money than driving one back and forth to Alaska or shipping one in and out for my annual adventures there.

MOTORCYCLE
ADVENTURER

CARL STEARNS CLANCY:
FIRST MOTORCYCLIST TO RIDE
AROUND THE WORLD 1912-1913

DR. GREGORY W. FRAZIER

The book Motorcycle Adventurer *recounts the first motorcycle ride around the world. Twenty-one-year-old Carl Stearns Clancy left New York in 1912 and returned 10 months later after having traveled 18,000 miles across North America, Europe, North Africa, and Asia.*

My research on global circumnavigations included one 16-year project to find and publish the true story about the first global circumnavigation. That was done by Carl Stearns Clancy in 1912–13 on a Henderson motorcycle. The result was my book *Motorcycle Adventurer* and a later publication titled *The Gasoline Tramp or Around the World on a Motorcycle*. An attempt to follow Clancy's original route 100 years after he had made his record-breaking ride was conceived by two Irish motorcycle enthusiasts and resulted in another book titled *In Clancy's Boots*. The Clancy ride around the globe was described at the time as "the longest, most difficult, and most perilous motorcycle journey ever attempted." One hundred years later, the Clancy adventure would still qualify as difficult, and given where he went, even today would be perilous in view of the political and religious climates and war zones on the planet.

Other publications by global circumnavigators on motorcycles have shed light on how they have seen the world they were traveling through. Nearly all tried to offer their personal insight after completing their long rides, as if they had experienced some epiphany along the way. Some would never make another long motorcycle ride. Others would go back to places they had passed through and capture the experience. For instance, Carl Stearns Clancy returned to Europe with moving picture cameras and a flamboyant actor by the name of Will Rogers. Clancy wrote, directed, and produced films with Rogers being in places where Clancy had been.

I have to admit that I have never had that earth-shaking enlightenment other global travelers claimed to have experienced while circling

I've stored a Kawasaki KMX200 in Southeast Asia for several years, using it for adventures in Thailand, Cambodia, and Malaysia.

I fashioned a custom survival toolkit above and beyond what came with the new motorcycle.

the planet. A female motorcyclist whose goal was to seek fame, fortune, and a green card to the United States by riding around the world once on her motorcycle challenged me when I declined her offer of marriage by retorting, "What are you going to do when you finish this trip, just keep riding around the world?"

"Why not?" was not the answer she wanted to hear.

Instead of continuously riding around the world on motorcycles, I have gone back many times to specific places on the globe that I liked. Other times I've been waylaid by red tape, though eventually found my way into (or out of) more sticky places around the globe. These extreme adventures included a great deal of planning, and included places seldom-seen from atop motorcycles by other American motorcycle travelers, places such as Myanmar (Burma), Cuba, and Vietnam.

In other instances I have returned to places I passed through on earlier rides and stayed for extensive periods, using comfortable places as base points for exploring surrounding countries or regions. I have done this in Europe numerous times, using Germany as my

Some places, such as this American Indian Tribal Reservation, appear to be impossible to enter on a solo basis. Countries such as Bhutan and Myanmar are similar.

base and storing motorcycles there for nearly 25 years. This allows me to fly into the country, spend time outfitting my equipment, and then roaming sometimes for hundreds of thousands of kilometers. I have stored motorcycles in South Africa, Alaska, Australia, South America, and Asia. It was far cheaper and more convenient to leave riding gear and the motorcycle for months, or years, in these countries rather than flying or shipping them in and out.

Storing motorcycles in a country and returning often also allows me to meet local people and immerse myself in the local expat communities. Three winters in Thailand using the Golden Triangle as a base found me part of the local expat motorcycling community in that part of the world. I would travel alone or with expats throughout Southeast Asia over the winters to neighboring countries such as Laos, Cambodia, and even into the Philippines. It was a comfortable way to spend winters while snow was flying half a world away back in Montana. It became too comfortable, though, and overwhelmed me a bit.

I made some difficult decisions that year about my circle of motorcycle friends. Living in an expat community such as Chiang Mai,

Thailand, or the larger area of Southeast Asia, brought me in contact with numerous motorcycle owners who passed through there or called it home. Some were good. Others, I learned, were not so good, and maybe that's likely why they were there. Expats with monikers such as Dave-the-Cuckold-Cop-Who-Writes-Like-an-Eighth-Grader and Bob's-the-Little-Fat-Man-Who-Took-the-Dale-Carnegie-Course-[*How To Win Friends and Influence People*]-and-Flunked-It-All-Three-Times had me looking at who was around me, who I was bonding with, and who were in my motorcycle owners' circle.

There were others, including the Ambivalent Rider, the Village Drool, the Financial Predator, the G-T Drunk, the Village-Big-Face-with-Little-It, the Village Wanker, the 7/11 Cheap Charlie, and the Village Khatoy Bum Bumper. It seemed too many lived a random existence without caring for love or truth, or a personal code of honor, and some were obvious miscreants. One longtime resident repeatedly told me he was the most important motorcyclist in Thailand, and then later wrote he lived in Thailand by a personal code of "*farang* rules don't apply here," meaning in his segment of the expat community, Western ethics, integrity, and honor were not standards by which he and his followers lived.

One of my major sponsors (along with several journalist colleagues) warned me, "If you sleep with dogs, you'll get fleas. Distance yourself." Their words of caution reminded me of one of the truer principles of life: "Once you get involved in the shit of another human, you become

Motorcycles were the most common form of motorized travel in the Land of Smiles, Thailand. I found the country to be motorcycle friendly and decided to return for a longer stay.

125

A "motorcycle-only" parking lot in Thailand at a major shopping mall. There was no room for my "big motorcycle" (600cc) with aluminum panniers, and I had to park outside.

magnetically attractive to the shit of others." Put another way, spend your time around the successful, and you will be successful.

I took heed. These were professional words of advice. I distanced myself and quit riding with most of them and drinking with them in their watering holes. I knew it was a small frog pond in which I had been croaking, but far smarter and wiser advisors showed me that the world was a much bigger pond. As one of the local motorcycling expats wrote, why hang out with assholes when there are so many nice people around?

It was fun to make a new circle of friends and I kept some of the old friends, respecting their personal principles, codes of honor, integrity, and intellect. One of the friendly frogs, then some of the culled reprobates and alcoholics from the distanced circle, cast me as the Eccentric Elitist, a moniker I happily accepted. I was not a misanthrope; I was being particular.

One of my older writing and riding friends said, "Look in the mirror, Greg. You suffer poorly motorcycle owners who are fools, misfits, grifters, financial predators, alcoholics, poseurs, incompetents, druggies, cut-rate parasites, scammers, leeches, liars, bullshitters, and Internet wankers. To those in that pond you are an elitist, an eccentric, because you prefer to ride alone and have survived more than a million miles and five loops around the globe doing so."

He was one of those rare men with a talent for original insight. I bristled at first, and then laughed with him, because he was right: I was an eccentric and an elitist. At least I had not been dubbed the Village Idiot.

Some of the global expat communities included social networks made up of motorcycle travelers who decided to stay rather than pass onward. Others returned later, buying local motorcycles or shipping in their own as I had.

I found collections of expat motorcycle adventurers from Kathmandu to Buenos Aires. The groups were usually not motorcycle brand-specific; they were mostly owners of mixed marques and sizes. Many were well-meaning motorcycle enthusiasts, meeting for dinners, day rides, and social events, sharing their experiences and camaraderie. Other members were not so good, however; they were

Catering to expatriates and tourists, this section of one town gave me a wakeup call of who and what were around me as fellow motorcyclists.

I explored the Golden Triangle in northern Thailand with one of the quality expat motorcyclists who taught me tricks to avoid being grifted, fleeced, or used by some Golden Triangle riders. He also taught me how to thank Buddha.

reprobates fleecing others to support their lifestyles. Some scored with their scheming methods in transferring money from my pocket. Here are a few examples:

The Sacred Ribbon Scam: The fleece-man stopped on a day ride at a church and told me all bikers stopped there for the sacred ribbons. He said the "blessed" ribbons were affixed to a traveler's motorcycle for safety and suggested I purchase several, for a donation to the church. I bought two for $5. Later I discovered he paid $1 for both and pocketed the $4 for beer money.

Pass the Helmet: At a motorcycle travelers' meeting, one local attendee asked if he could "pass the helmet" to raise money for a local motorcycle mechanic jailed in a nearby country where donated money bought basic needs such as soap and clothes, and $700 was raised. Later, an emissary was sent with $700 to the prison and attested to the amount he delivered. What was not known (except to the grifter) was how much the family of the prisoner had added to the overall amount and how much was pocketed by the grifter as his collection fee.

Monk Money: A group of local motorcyclists planted two trees at a church in memory of two of their fallen motorcycle friends. An annual memorial ride followed, stopping for the night in the town where the church was, where everyone hoisted a few drinks in memory of their friends. The leader suggested donating money to the monks for taking care of the trees and offered to collect and deliver the funds. The next morning, when the donation box was inspected, no funds had been deposited. The grifter's life of swilling had been financed by the unknowing motorcycle sheep being fleeced by a two-legged leech.

Kick-Back Boots: The newbie to a local expat community asked a longtime motorcycle resident for a recommendation of where to purchase new motorcycle boots. Not only did the expat have a suggestion, but he offered to escort the newbie to the shop where a custom pair of leather riding boots could be made. As the newbie neither spoke the local language nor knew what a fair price was, he quickly agreed. At the shop, a deal was struck, and all parted happily. When the newbie went to collect his new boots, the shop owner advised him there was an additional 1,000 Thai baht (about $30 USD) required. As my acquaintance related this tale, he laughed, saying the boots

These are the original boots worn by Carl Stearns Clancy during his 1912–13 record-setting ride around the world. These boots were carried 100 years later on the Clancy Centenary Ride by a BMW GS rider and presented to Dr. Gregory Frazier, who donated them to the National Motorcycle Museum.

These are the original Thai "kick-back" boots sold to a newbie rider by his trusted "kick-back" guide.

I had to make some tough decisions while spending time in Thailand, such as who I wanted in my circle of motorcycling acquaintances and who I did not, earning me the moniker of the Eccentric Elitist for not wanting to associate with some who were using me.

were his "kick-back boots," not for kicking back as in relaxing, but as in the kick-back for the local grifter who delivered him to the shop like a fish to be filleted.

Best Rate Money Changer: I was about to enter a bank in Peru to change dollars when an expat sitting on a parked Honda said, "Inside they'll make you wait, and then give you a low rate. I can give you a better rate." Too good to be true, I passed, but my traveling pal chose to swap his $100 bill for some of the local biker's bills. Everyone was smiles until my pal tried to pay for lunch with some of his new money. It was counterfeit, all of it. We went back to the bank to see if we could hunt down the swindler. Of course he was long gone, living that day on the new Ben Franklin he had gotten for cheap.

Computing the Check: I was clipped several times by an expert who lived on small change. He was a welcoming expat motorcyclist who spoke the local language well enough to order off the menu. When the bill was presented to us as a group, he would take it from the waitress and then tell each of us how much our share was. I was fleeced several times before I saw a bill and did the math myself, having learned the currency rates and written amounts. The chiseler had been eating and drinking for free off me and others by spreading his portions across our respective percentages.

Hotel Scam Man: An expat offered to organize a ride for a group of us. Because he spoke the local language, he would enter the hotel first, check on room status, then come out and tell us if they had rooms available and how much each would cost. We would check in,

I was told that sleeping with dogs begets fleas. I decided to stay away.

pay, and figure we were getting a deal. Later, when I checked into the same hotel on my own, I learned the "good old boy" price the leader had negotiated was far more than a normal walk-in paid. The hotel paid a cash commission to the scammer, offering me the same deal if I brought in a group of friends.

When I was expressing my disdain for the expat motorcycle grifters and con men and lack of respect for their character, one of my colleagues suggested I grant the scammers some respect. I replied, "What do you mean, grant them some respect? They are pond scum, feeding off the naive and trusting motorcycle travelers passing through or sucking them into their websites for fleecing."

"Respect that they have been scamming for years," he replied. "It's their profession, and many are very good at it. You were conned by some of the best."

I fought back with, "A prostitute as a professional, I respect. I'd lend money to a prostitute, not so some third-world motorcycle owner who stiffed me for a free meal or beer money. Hey, wait, I did lend money to a prostitute once, and got it back. Not so for the slippery snollygoster in the Land of Smiles who called himself the media contact for the local motorcycle club. He still owes me $175 and is overdue a grifter adventure."

Being part of these expat communities—whether using them as a base or just passing through them—had given me a perspective on motorcycle owners and drivers that became jaded, but over a period of 30 years I concluded it was part of the price I had to pay for taking my motorcycling to extremes and for not being content to stay on one continent. I still laugh at myself at how naïve I had been and how I was *still* hooked by a friendly smile or offer of assistance while in pursuit of adventure.

Traveling by motorcycle, like being in business, involves risk. An acceptable degree of comfort varies for each of us, as does our ability to afford the risk of loss. While one traveler feels little risk driving solo through Russia or the jungles of Brazil, the next would not consider doing the same unless in an armed convoy. The same could be said of the college graduate with an MBA who decides China is where he wants to make a living versus another graduate who takes a secure job in a government agency.

My advice to motorcyclists who want to push their personal adventuring envelopes is this: accept risk and danger as elements in the adventure equation, then manage those factors within your control to reduce the degree of risk.

My experience for managing risk began with mechanical maintenance. As a newbie, my motorcycle's well-being was far down my checklist of risk-management items as long as the motorcycle started and moved forward. The first well-used big motorcycle I owned was an abused and road-weary 1945 Indian Chief that would move forward under its own power once the ignition was turned. Mechanical failures often left me stranded on the side of some desolate road in Wyoming or Montana, however. Those unscheduled pit stops taught me how to repair a flat tire by carrying the right tools and a patch kit. I also added other tools, nuts, bolts, and electrical wire to that kit for additional repairs. I learned that the axiom, an ounce of prevention was worth a pound of cure, was true, so I began doing routine maintenance and inspections before adventuring away from my base. By prepping the motorcycle, I found I could avoid spending another afternoon in the hot sun fabricating cable from fence wire and bailing twine that would open and close the throttle. Doing routine inspections and maintenance was reducing my risk of experiencing memorable but not so enjoyable roadside repairs.

I have returned to the business of managing motorcycle maintenance numerous times over the last 40 years. I have done so by adding to my toolkit(s) new items such as glues, hose clamps, cable ties, and motorcycle-specific special tools. I have also constructed a mobile repair kit that I take with me from country to country when renting or purchasing unknown motorcycles for short-term adventures. With it, I was once able to reduce my risk of spending a long afternoon in the jungles of Cambodia by using vice grips to stretch tired springs on a Yamaha with a slipping clutch.

Down again! Here, I entertained the villagers who saw me make a slight get-off, as well as laughed at myself for picking such a public place to display my motorbike piloting skills. A dog had darted in front of me, and while trying to avoid it, the front wheel washed out.

The risk of losing or having stolen valuables such as cash, credit cards, a driver's license, and a passport is as high while touring the United States as it is in Morocco or Serbia. I learned to carry my VIP documents, papers, and cash well away from those needed for daily use. I carry two wallets and a third waterproof document holder for the extremely valuable papers. In my "decoy" wallet the thief or finder will discover only enough folding money to get me through the day and one credit or ATM card. They will also find a plastic-coated color copy of my driver's license, some business cards, and a couple of important-looking documents such as an expired international driving permit, dead telephone card, and a nonactivated frequent flyer card. Each day I use this replenished wallet to pay for my expected expenses. If it is stolen or lost, I need only be frantic about the loss of the one credit card, which means one telephone call, and I have some solace in knowing my others are safely stashed within my regular wallet. I keep the decoy wallet somewhere on my body where it is easy for me to get to, such as an outside jacket pocket. The wallet with the good stuff I keep hidden well away from my decoy.

The management of risk applies to swilling and chilling with the locals. I have a mental savings account filled with stories of motorcycle travelers who have met physical harm and more after joining a group of locals for a night on the town. An example is of one of my motorcycle friends who could only last remember being in the lobby of his hotel with two ladies after meeting them in a bar when he woke

Besides hunting fun roads to ride, I also hunt opportunities to fish. This 100-pound Mekong catfish was only out of the water long enough to take the photo, and then we returned it to the pond for another fisherman to catch.

up the next day in his hotel room, robbed of everything valuable. It was a quality hotel and the security videos showed him laughing and drinking with his guests in the lobby. His loss of memory and headache told him and the police he had been drugged. When I asked him what cost him the most that night, his loss of dignity or loss of valuables, he answered it was the loss of his expensive electronic motorcycle key, which took nearly a week to replace. His big money, passport, and other important items had been securely locked in the hotel safe that night.

If I remember adventure travel has a lot in common with business, maybe I can increase the return on my investment. In other words, over time I will enjoy more the benefits of my pursuits, even though it can be a risky business.

Some of my adventures around the planet could be called little more than a weekend ride, while others were serious expeditions. When asked why I pushed my personal envelopes for risk and financial ruin for the sake of experiencing some place while riding a motorcycle, I thought to where my adventure envelope was compared to those asking and came to some conclusions.

Who would want to be a serious adventure seeker? As a global motorcycle wanderer I met numerous motorcycle travelers who were self-proclaimed adventure riders. Some sported stickers on their helmets, panniers, and motorcycles to proclaim their commitment to what appeared to be their hobby.

Once, I was in a motorcycle shop when a customer walked in and asked the owner if he knew the motorcyclist who had ridden through China and Burma, a motorcycle traveler the customer said was "a real adventure rider." The shop owner did not know who or where the real adventure rider was, but after the customer was out of earshot, asked me, "You've been described as 'America's no. 1 extreme adventure rider.' What makes a motorcycle traveler a real adventure rider?"

I laughed, and said, "I believe it's like beauty, an image in the eye of the beholder."

Curious, I pondered what could be the factors that make up what was under the façade of stickers, riding gear, avatars, and equipment, and then some of the theories supporting those factors. More simply defined, what is the difference in the DNA of an adventure rider versus that of a motorcycle owner, driver, or traveler?

When I was roadracing motorcycles, there was a theory floating that the go-fast guys had a higher level of adrenaline in their systems, giving the front runners a higher degree of ferocity. This gave the winners an apparent fearlessness, allowing them to go deeper into the turns before braking, making riskier passes, upping the rpms a few more revolutions before shifting, and generally pushing their limits further than the other racers.

After moving off the paved racecourses and onto gravel and dirt, some of the wild men in my new circle of racing motorcyclists suggested the difference between the winners and losers was "monkey gland juice," an exotic liquid only procured from wild monkey secretions. This theory was discounted as motorcycle racing male buffalo excreta. I never saw a professional racer using an eye dropper to dribble it on his or her tongue or take secret monkey pills before a race or serious off-road ride. What I concluded was talent, mixed with luck, made the man or woman a winner or loser.

Over my lifetime as a motorcycle traveler and racer I have had some good luck and a "bit of talent," according to some of my sponsors. I would like to again experience some of the levels of barrel-of-monkey fun I experienced as a far younger and faster motorcycle traveler and pilot.

Cuban motorcyclists met me upon my arrival in Havana and entertained me with their tales of motorcycles and lifestyles in Cuba.

Cuba Extreme: Hemingway, Cigars, and Old Motorcycles

In Havana, I met a toilet saleswoman.

A woman hawking Cuban cigars followed me into a public toilet. She was a tough saleslady, bent on extracting as many dollars from me as possible. I badly needed to relieve myself but could not convince her to leave. I was probably the only Norte Americano she had met who did not smoke—who in fact had an allergy to smoke, especially cigar smoke. The hard part was telling her in Spanish, of which I speak little. I tried, using words such as, "No cigar," and fluttering my hands to shoo her away, then pointing at my crotch and saying, "*Necessario*!" Her eyes lit up, she smiled, and said, "*Si, como Presidente Clinton y Monika*." Relief finally came when a stall door opened and the occupant exited. I slipped past him, away from the female who I was not sure was at that point offering to sell me sex or a Cuban cigar. Maybe both.

Ernest Hemingway lived in Cuba for nearly 20 years and wanted to stay there for 20 more. After Fidel Castro and Che Guevara, Hemingway was, and possibly is, the best-known personality associated with the island. Ernesto was forced to leave Cuba in 1960 when the United States broke relations with the country, but he always expected to return. The house he owned, Finca Vigia (Lookout Farm), was opened to the public in 1994, and for an entrance fee (plus an additional fee for each camera), I viewed how it was when he left. Worn shoes and boots were still on the floor of the closet, where hung numerous shirts, pants, and jackets. Toothbrushes and razors were hanging in their holders in the bathroom. The most telling items left behind were a pair of glasses, his typewriter, and 8,000 to 9,000 books. It has been suggested his inability to return contributed to his depression, which ultimately resulted in sticking the barrel of a shotgun in his mouth and splattering his award-winning gray matter over the walls and ceiling of the entry hallway of his second house in Ketchum, Idaho, in 1961.

I am guilty of being a Hemingway cultist. I did not appreciate the man or his work when he was required reading in high school or college. It was years later, when I was in a small bar in the town of Big Horn, Wyoming, that I took an interest in him. Until that time I did not know Hemingway spent considerable time in the Big Horn Mountains. He stayed at a guest ranch near Big Horn, hunted and drank with the locals, and crashed his car one night, ending up in our hospital in Billings, Montana. I learned he often worked in the Big Horn. My interest was piqued, learning that such a gifted writer would choose this part of the world to relax or work on some of his best books. He seldom wrote about the Big Horn Mountain area, so prior to that time I knew little of our local resident Nobel and Pulitzer

Cuba means old motorcycles and old cars, still running and not in museums, a tribute to the tenacity and creativeness of owners unable to purchase spare or replacement parts due to an embargo around the country.

There really were old cars in Cuba. The sad side was most were patched together with bits off of everything from tractors to boat parts.

One rental I found was this Jupiter with sidecar. It was a two-stroke Russian model, and rental included the driver, who was needed to clear several road checks. I could have bought the outfit, but the owner and I could not figure out how I could make the paperwork in my name, so I passed on doing that deal for the three weeks.

Prize winner. Barfly residents told me he was viewed as "one of them," albeit always a visitor.

Traveling around Cuba, the most popular picture I saw was of Che. The second most popular was that of Fidel. Number three was Papa, as Hemingway was fondly nicknamed. Throughout the Havana area were tourist points for aficionados to taste a little Hemingway: a room in a local hotel, touting "Ernesto slept here!" or the Restaurante Floridita, said to be a haunt of the author, charging $6 for a daiquiri and $7 for a chicken sandwich. And finally there was Gregorio Fuentes, pilot of Hemingway's boat the *Pilar*. In early 2002, Fuentes passed away, at age 104. Friends of Fuentes say he never read any of Hemingway's works, with him claiming, "What for? I've lived them with him." Fuentes and Hemingway bonded over 30 years, and speculators said Fuentes was the model for Santiago in *The Old Man and*

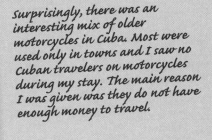

Surprisingly, there was an interesting mix of older motorcycles in Cuba. Most were used only in towns and I saw no Cuban travelers on motorcycles during my stay. The main reason I was given was they do not have enough money to travel.

Seen on the streets in Havana were a number of odd-looking motorcycles from a number of foreign countries, the most being from Russia.

the Sea. One tourist book mentioned that Fuentes' son was charging $50 for a 15-minute consultation with the old man.

I came to Cuba to do research on the Indians (people, not motor-cycles) of the island. Given my passion for motorcycles, however, it was hard not to spend time looking at the old motorcycles used daily for everything from taxis to farm machines. The Russian Urals and Jupiters, pre-1959 (when the U.S. embargo went into effect), were the workhorses in this living museum for old machinery, while the old flathead and panhead Harley-Davidsons were what made dreams for men, both young and old. Had Hemingway lived to return to Cuba, he may have noted the feelings Cubans had for motorcycles and penned *The Young Man and the Motorcycle*. Had he done so, I would have taken an interest in him and his works far sooner than I did.

A visit to the home Ernest Hemingway left for what he thought to be a short time was found it as it was in 1960.

This sign reminds visitors of the Indian rebels.

Riding a motorcycle in Cuba was a breeze compared to our daily commutes or weekend rides in the United States. The road system, while better than India or Central America, presented any speed demon with an obstacle course of potholes, rail crossings, and "sleeping policemen" (speed bumps) that easily waffled a front-wheel rim or bottomed out a suspension if hit at a velocity of more than 50 miles per hour.

I roamed freely throughout Cuba, but was stopped several times by traffic police and asked to show ownership papers for the motorcycle. I saw only two motorcyclists wearing helmets, and one was a football helmet. The motorcycle police, though, all wore helmets, and when I asked a local motorcyclist why the people didn't wear them, he said, "We cannot afford them." With an average monthly salary of around $20, there is not much left after beans and rice to purchase a motorcycle, let alone a helmet.

Cuba was a bastion of communism, yet capitalism has grown like a weed. For instance, there exists a secondary market for sleeping rooms outside of the government-owned hotels called the *casas particulares*. These are best likened to a small German *gasthaus*, or private house whose owner rents out a spare room. The average nightly price was $25, although I paid less when away from the big cities. One owner told me he paid $250 each month to the government for his license, and the government set the rate for his room rental. Where capitalism entered the economics of this system was when the owner sold the guest a meal, beer, or soda. I asked for a beer one night, and the owner sent his daughter to the market, where she paid 85 cents for the bottle, for which he charged me $1. A large dinner cost $5. None of these transactions were reported to the government, because they weren't allowed under the owner's government license—only room rental was. This owner, filled with entrepreneur spirit, gave me a handful of business cards to "give to my friends" when I departed.

What I did not understand about the U.S.-Cuba relationship and politics is why the United States believes the 50-year-old embargo works. Maybe it did 30 years ago, making life hard on the Cuban people in hopes of them rising up and overthrowing their government. Part of the U.S. policy was to squeeze our trading partners and political friends around the world into not doing business with Cuba. That pressure has been ignored. The police ride Moto Guzzi motorcycles from Italy. Yamaha, Suzuki, and Honda motorcycles from Japan can be seen there, as can Heineken beer and German electrical components. In an average Havana street bar, I saw Carlsberg, Bavaria, and Corona beers on the menu, and JB scotch and Jack Daniels whiskey on the shelf. The politicos in Washington, D.C., know far more than

I had some fun exploring a number of public military displays. When asked where I was from by officials at some of the museums, I would avoid extended conversations by saying I was from Canada, not wanting to engage in discussions about U.S. and Cuban relations.

Castro slept here. A museum in a former prison had signs, some with photographs, over the beds where the rebels were first housed after their failed attempt to overthrow the government. Castro spent a year here before he left Cuba.

I do about why the United States insists on squeezing Cuba, but my thumbnail economic and political analysis is our policies have made Cuban life harder, but the resolution of the people stronger.

The Cubans were much friendlier than I thought they would be. Like the Brazilians, they like to laugh, make jokes, dance, tap their feet to a good musical beat, and do not take themselves too seriously. Through my motorcycle world, I was lucky enough to meet a Cuban BSA owner who invited me to his home for dinner. He said I would meet Barbarito Torres, the member of the Buena Vista Social Club who played the strange, 12-string small guitar (*laud*) in the movie *Buena Vista Social Club*. Before leaving for Cuba, I was instructed to watch their video and listen to their music. It was an interesting dinner. While Torres told me stories in Spanish (which were interpreted by his manager), recounting his bus tour around the United States and sharing a laugh, we toasted our mutual dislike of snow and cold in towns such as Telluride and Aspen, Colorado. It never snows in Cuba.

My hosts in Cuba were a fun-loving bunch. They seemed apolitical and our commonality was motorcycles, which transcended any political differences.

I was invited to a show the next night at Hostale Valencia. Torres and his band were a musical highlight of my Cuban adventure, with a crowd of 50 stuffed into a room suited for 40. It was far better than the CD or movie. My right foot still moves up and down when reflecting on that evening.

Motorcyclists welcomed me to Cuba. The Latin American Motorcycle Association (LAMA) adopted me. I walked out of the airport in Havana, expecting to be met by one member. Instead, there were a dozen bikers, including the local chapter president. I was overwhelmed by LAMA members, their wives and girlfriends, all wearing the LAMA colors and riding pre-1959 motorcycles. I was shaken, not expecting anything like a reception. They whisked me into town, secured a *hostal*, and set up a schedule for riding and

The most popular sign anywhere in Cuba were those of Che Guevara. He was seemingly held in higher esteem than any political leaders, alive or long since dead.

photography that included a club party, Sunday ride, and a borrowed motorcycle. It was humbling to be treated so well by a group of total strangers. I was quickly learning about Cubans, their hospitality, and motorcycling in this land 90 miles south of Miami. Mario Nieves, international president of LAMA, had told me the Cuban bikers were "good people." He was right, but I would say "great people."

The Indians I was looking for never appeared. That was a tough assignment. It seems when the Spanish invaded the island, their solution to the "Indian Problem" was much like that of the British when dealing with the Aborigines of Australia on Tasmania or the Americans: wipe them out if they do not conform.

The Indians of Cuba put up a fight. Their resistance leader was Hatuey, a rebel like Fidel Castro, who was skilled in guerrilla warfare. Like Castro, Hatuey was captured. Unlike Castro, who ended up in prison for a couple of years, Hatuey was burned at the stake in 1512.

History says that as the flames were sizzling the skin off Hatuey, the Spaniard Father Jaun de Tesin offered baptism with the promise that if baptized, the rebel chieftain would go to Heaven. The chief asked the father if Spaniards went to Heaven when they died. When the priest confirmed Heaven would have Spaniards, Hatuey declined baptism, saying he did not want to be with such "cruel and wicked people as Christians." Chief Joseph, Sitting Bull, Plenty Coups, and Hatuey probably all ended in the place where wise men go after leaving this time and planet. I suspect in the happy cosmos they met and sucked down a cool drink, the one named after Hatuey in Cuba, a malt without alcohol.

CHAPTER EIGHT

BURMA

Adventuring the Hard and Easy Way in Myanmar

"No! You cannot ride a motorcycle in Myanmar! Foreigners not allowed! No visa today!"

So said the immigration official at the Myanmar Embassy in Bangkok. His firm dismissal of my request was followed by a rapid flipping of the back of his left hand at me to go away from the "Foreigner" visa application window. This was not my first indicator (merely another reminder) that getting into the country and traveling by motorcycle were going to be hard.

Myanmar (formerly called Burma) was one of the dark countries on the globe for overland motorcycle travelers. Motorcycling through the country has long been thought to be impossible. One couple managed to cross the country but only by extensive use of trucks to carry their motorcycle through "forbidden zones," large sections of the country where foreigners are not allowed enter.

Several years earlier, I had managed a short ride into Myanmar from Thailand before being stopped and escorted *back* to Thailand by armed military goons. I crossed into Myanmar at the small border town of Tachilek on a Thai rental bike. Once inside, I rode to the first checkpoint, not far from the border. There, the pole across the road was up, the guards were sleeping, and I rode through thinking, "I'm in." At the next checkpoint, the guards were awake and one stood in the middle of the road with his rifle in front of a metal pole that crossed the road.

I played the dumb tourist, but it got me no farther up the road. Instead, two guards escorted me back to the border in a small pickup. While one guard drove the truck behind me, the other stood in the bed of the pickup with his rifle pointed forward. I sensed the guys were serious about where I should not have been, but at the same time I broke up a monotonous day and gave them a chance to head into town for the night instead of spending it at the lonely jungle post.

I was given a stern lecture at the border by the immigration officials; they said they could confiscate my motorcycle as well as all of my possessions. They could also fine me and toss me in jail and there would be no call to the American embassy for help or notification because the United States did not have one in Myanmar. They let me leave but warned me not to come back. I was *persona non grata*. I did notice they had no computers in their office; maybe my name would not appear at a later date when I returned.

Three years later, I had a new plan. I learned there were motorcycles in Myanmar. My plan was to fly into the center of Myanmar with my riding gear and beg, borrow, steal, rent, or buy whatever I could find, then ride around the country.

My first barrier was getting a visa. At the Myanmar Embassy in Bangkok, they were issuing only 60 to 100 visas per day, and the application line started at 1 a.m. The doors opened at 9 a.m. I arrived at 6 a.m. only to be told to come back the next day after waiting until 11 a.m.; they were taking no more applications. Then I went to the application window and asked about riding in Myanmar.

When I left the embassy, I noticed a food wagon just outside the entrance gate that had a box of passports from different countries. The seller was handing them out to certain runners who came to her food wagon. The light dawned on me.

The visa application process was slow because the immigration office processed all applications by hand; they didn't use computers. In the morning they would receive 60 to 100 visas, then they would process them in the afternoon. The next morning they would give the passports back to the applicants with the new visas in them. Paid runners with piles of passports and applications would line up next to the food seller's stall and the gate, as the food seller had the best spot.

I talked to her in my very limited Thai. With great trepidation I gave her my passport, a completed Report on Arrival Myanmar Immigration form with a photo attached, plus $40. She promised that in two days, saying, "1,000 percent sure," she would have my $20 visa for the $20 handling fee.

For the next two days I questioned whether my adventure into Myanmar had already been an impossible (or stupid) one, having handed over my passport to an unknown food seller on the street, plus $40 cash. But two days later, I landed in Yangon, Myanmar, with my passport—with a valid visa in hand—plus my helmet, riding gear, and a wad of American dollars to secure a motorcycle.

Yangon, formally known as Rangoon, was a "forbidden area" for motorcycles save for military or government officials. The city had been a former capital of Myanmar and the government had outlawed motorcycles because of their utility in drive-by assassinations with one person driving, the other shooting from the back. The government also outlawed all bicycles in the same area, except for those used with postal delivery. When the government built a new capital farther inland, they left the laws intact for Yangon.

With some help from a motorcycle travel friend from Germany, I found a travel agency that claimed it knew where a motorcycle could be rented in Yangon. It was a private deal—cash only. The owner of the motorcycle was the proprietor of a teashop and owned a couple of bikes. He had been a motorcycle dealer before the government had outlawed motorcycles and put him out of business. He still loved them, though, and had three or four bikes. For $3,000 he had bought a Honda XR250 in pieces in 1999 and cobbled it together for a runner. With a cash deposit of $1,000 and $35 per day, I could rent the Honda. However, he had to charge me another $25 to take the motorcycle and me in a truck 25 miles out of town, outside the forbidden area and drop me off, then collect me at the same point when I returned. There was no signed rental agreement, no insurance, and only a copy of my passport and a handshake to seal the deal, which included my agreement to pay him another $2,000 if the motorcycle were confiscated by road police or anyone else.

Another interesting quirk in Yangon was there were no gasoline stations in the city proper. The government deemed them unsafe. To top

off the Honda we stopped at a busy gasoline station outside the city, and after that the owner told me I was on my own. He gave me his cell phone number to call one hour before I returned to the city so he could send the truck out to where I was and collect the motorcycle and me.

Before leaving his shop I wanted to test the bike, because when I first saw it, the poor thing was in parts and not running. He assembled it and I made a quick run up and down the block while his helpers kept an eye out for police. It ran, the brakes worked, and the clutch found all the gears. By the time I was on my own, I figured I had already broken at least a dozen laws. I dreaded losing $3,000, but I had spent three years buying into this adventure so I was committed.

Within the first 75 miles I ran into a government checkpoint. My blood pressure moved into the red zone as the uniformed officer with a big gun signaled me to stop. He spoke no English, and my Burmese was limited to a smile, but I understood he wanted to see my passport when he held out his hand and demanded, in French, "Papiers." I played the stupid tourist, then tried to bury him with paperwork by giving him a copy of my International Driving Permit, a laminated color photocopy of my driver's license, a color copy of an old U.S. motorcycle title and registration, and half a dozen business cards and motorcycle stickers. I kept my cash and credit cards out of sight.

Ten minutes of thumbing through my passport, shuffling papers, and talking with his subordinates got him to a point where he did not know what to do with me. He pulled a hand-written ledger out of a desk drawer, wrote down my name and passport number, then the city where I pointed on a map was my destination. He kept the stickers at my insistence, but gave me back everything else and wished me safe travels toward my destination. Maybe someday another motorcycle

I tried to sneak into Myanmar through some small dirt roads in northern Thailand, but I was turned back at a jungle border. It would take me three more attempts years later before I was eventually able to figure out how to ride a motorcycle in Myanmar.

traveler will be stopped there and see my personalized sticker on the wall. Send me an email if you do. I'd like to know how you made out in Myanmar.

The road surfaces varied from new concrete to bombed-out and potholed crushed rock. Traffic was light and there were some small motorcycles on the road, 100–110cc Chinese copies of Hondas and Yamahas. My 250cc Honda was a big bike and attracted attention whenever I stopped, as did my riding gear and helmet. Because of the tropical temperature and humidity in this part of the world, helmets are called "rice cookers." They cost $2 to $10 and are made of some beanie-style eggshell-like composition. My Nolan helmet was possibly the most expensive and best-constructed helmet many of the local motorcycle riders had ever seen.

The next challenge was gasoline. The first stop was at a place where I spotted 5-gallon plastic containers by the side of the road, next to which there was plenty of oil-covered dirt and some funnels. The process was for me to tell the owner how many liters I wanted, which he would pour out of the 5-gallon plastic container into a metal liter container with a pour spout. He then stuck a large funnel in my gas tank and put a piece of a T-shirt inside the funnel to use as a filter. He computed the cost on his fingers and I handed him as many bills as I though he meant, which averaged about $4 per gallon.

In the larger towns I purchased gasoline at regular gas stations, usually located at the outskirts of town. In the countryside it was gas from the plastic containers. Several times when I offered too much money, the sellers would hand me back my mistake. Not once did I sense I was being taken advantage of, but that has a lot to do with the Buddhist culture of most of the population. I felt the same honesty in restaurants and hotels or guesthouses where I stayed.

Traffic moved slowly due to the varied road conditions and the quality and age of the vehicles; none were new. The fact that slower speeds meant less gas consumption in a poor country likely also contributed to the slower pace. The one exception was a new Mercedes bearing diplomatic license plates that passed me at well over 100 miles per hour. I averaged 25 miles per hour the first two days. After that I quit computing mileage or average speed, concerning myself more with finding gasoline and places to eat and sleep.

In 1973, the country changed to driving on the right side of the road. The change was made because most of the cars came from Japan and had the steering wheel on the left side. The most difficult part of riding was reading the road signs, which were in Burmese, especially in cities. Staying with the larger flow of traffic was usually the right choice— that, and keeping an eye on the sun and knowing which direction I wanted to go. I purchased a road map in Yangon that featured the larger roads on it but none of the ones in the countryside.

Riding north to Mandalay was not possible; there were large forbidden zones in between. I had to truck the motorcycle through those areas and book a flight for myself over them. Even Burmese nationals who were not residents of the area were not allowed to travel through the zones. They were like restricted military bases in the United States, only much larger.

The Honda and I floated back to Yangon on a slow ferry. At the dock, the owner was waiting with his workers. One worker pushed the motorcycle back to the teashop a mile away, while the owner and I took a taxi. When the final bill was computed, the owner gave me back my $1,000 deposit and then asked to be paid in new, unfolded, $100 bills, which I had. We parted friends—fellow motorcyclists in a dark part of the world for motorcycle riders—a place where it was against the law to even honk or beep a horn. I suggested I might return someday, this time to ride south and maybe on into Thailand. For that, I'd have to purchase the motorcycle, which he said he would gladly sell to me.

The flight to Mandalay, my next destination, was inexpensive. It was on a turbo prop plane that shook more taking off or landing than the Honda XR250 did on a bad road. The city was teeming with small motorcycles, the preferred method of transportation. A new Chinese-made 110–125 step-through model could be purchased for $450 and up. While there were a few bigger bikes around, most were older or smuggled in by someone well connected with the military leaders. One BMW 600cc bike went by, but that was being piloted by a police officer.

The hunt for a rental motorcycle was fruitless on the Internet, proving again that all the answers and information in the world are not on there. Instead, a moneychanger on the street who spoke English said he knew someone who rented bikes. He told me to come back to the same corner in an hour and a couple of motorcycles would be there for inspection.

I tried both a 125cc and a 110cc. Afterward, I was led down a small alley to a private house where the moneychanger translated the deal between the owner and me. The rental cost $12 per day without deposit, but I had to give the owner a copy of my passport and half of the rental amount up front, in new, unfolded U.S. dollars again. The owner also asked me to write by hand the rental agreement, which said I agreed to rent the bike for $12 per day, and write my name and passport number on the paper. He couldn't read my hand-printed English, neither could the moneychanger, but when I handed him the money and a copy of my passport he carefully folded everything together and handed it to his wife. She and the rest of his family, including his mother, sister, and several children, had been called into the room to observe the whole transaction, his way of showing "big face" in doing a business deal with a white foreigner.

The gas tank was nearly full and tire pressure close to what it should have been. There was even some tread on the tires. It had an electric starter but came with no tools or ownership papers. When I asked the moneychanger about the lack of tools, he said I should not worry, "Everybody will help you."

Driving in the north was similar to the south, except for the mountain range I went over. On a series of switchbacks, a tanker truck carrying gasoline broke down, causing a 100- to 200-vehicle jam in both directions. I was able to weave in and out of the hundreds of vehicles on my little bike, which saved me from a three- to four-hour wait while a tow truck and the police tried to clear the road. Had I been on a big bike, with luggage on the sides in saddlebags or aluminum boxes, I would have had to sit there with the cars and trucks.

The upside to the Chinese bike was it got two or three times the mileage per gallon than the Honda XR250. The downside was it was much slower and the seat was a butt-buster. After two days, there was no way I could sit on the seat without experiencing severe bun pain.

When the bike died in a small town, a passerby used his cell phone to call a mechanic who determined the spark plug was dead. He replaced it with a used one, adjusted the carburetor and chain, and then checked the brake cables and spokes. The final bill for the roadside assistance was 80 cents, less than a dollar an hour, and that included the replacement spark plug.

The little bike kept up with all other vehicles on the road except for the numerous "taxi cars" that ferried backpackers and tourists at breakneck speeds far exceeding road and equipment conditions.

I thanked Buddha I was not inside a taxi with the crazed pilot when one passed me in either direction, thinking either he would maim me or I him.

People were friendly everywhere, whether at a restaurant or gas stop. They were often surprised to discover I was an American, and one curious university student asked to have her picture taken with me. Besides the United States having an embargo around the country, America has very poor relations with the Myanmar government. At the people level, however, all seemed gentle and prayerful and talk of politics was generally shunned. One English-speaking guide who invited himself to walk with me around a pagoda lamented that he could be thrown in jail for discussing politics and democracy, the topics he tried most to discuss, and those that I begged off entering into.

Many of the tourists I met were from France or Italy, and smaller numbers were from Germany. I met only one other American in my three weeks of travel, a single female tourist in a hotel elevator.

News was hard to find. My winter home of Thailand (Myanmar's neighbor) had just experienced a military coup, and I was uncertain how I would find things when I returned, or if I could return at all. Access to the Internet was dreadfully slow, and many sites were blocked by the Myanmar government, especially news websites. Once in a while I could find an Internet café where the owner was savvy enough to know how to get around the blocks and get me connected with my Yahoo account. The connection was slow, however, and it often took up to 10 minutes to open a file or e-mail. I finally gave up trying to connect.

In hotels, if the room had a television, the two or three stations were bland, running cartoons, old movies, or government news. The fashion channel, though, seemed popular.

Government-controlled newspapers had only good news, but they were written in Burmese, which I could not read, so it mattered little that I wanted the bad news too. I finally gave up on trying to keep up with the outside world or even what was happening inside Myanmar. I focused instead on my daily survival on the road, dodging potholes, trucks in my lane, and the insane drivers of the errant taxis. Sadly, my mother passed away while I was in the Myanmar dark world of limited news and Internet. I did not find out about her passing until I returned to Thailand and was able to access my e-mail account, a week after she was gone.

My last days in Myanmar were bikeless. The places I wanted to see were unreachable on my Mandalay rental motorcycle, so I returned it to the owner. After that I played tourist, using my cameras to record things such as the largest bell in the world, pagodas, and Mount Popa.

In New Bagan I tried, unsuccessfully, to rent or buy a motorcycle. Tourist travel in that town, known for its 8,000 temples or pagodas, was limited to walking, rental bicycles, or one-horse carriages. I was not a happy motorcycle adventurer and soon discovered my great dislike for the barefoot walking in temples or climbing of pagodas, shoes and socks not being allowed.

The last day in Mandalay was spent taking photographs of motorcycles on the street. The British had left a great number of BSA motorcycles in Burma when they pulled out of the country. I was led to believe many of the old singles were still running around, but I found only one. It seems the Brits lust for these old bikes. Entrepreneurs had flown into the country and purchased nearly all the old British bikes they could find and shipped the lot back to Great Britain.

Over the previous 10 years, I had tried to ride through Myanmar from the west side (Bangladesh) and the east side (Thailand). Each attempt had been thwarted by government rules and forbidden zones. The idea of riding and trucking my motorcycle across the country while I hopped across in airplanes did not seem like much of an adventure. My ride inside the country was as close as I was going to get to roaming independently by motorcycle. In the end it was a great adventure, but a hard one. Now that I know how to do it, I may go back. The political situation and my personal adventure-seeking meter will determine that decision.

In 2013, I was told some foreign motorcyclists had managed to cross the border successfully into Myanmar from Thailand and ride their motorcycles free within the country. The bragging rights were being claimed by a group of five foreign riders who cyber-shouted they were the first to ride big motorcycles into Myanmar in December 2012. Their claim piqued my interest, and I thought maybe the country was opening up and I could take my own big bike into Myanmar from Thailand.

The country had long been difficult to enter by motorcycle. Difficult but not impossible. For those wanting to check Burma off their ultimate motorcycling adventure-riding bucket list, a day pass allowed riders, on any displacement motorcycle, to exit Thailand at Mae Sai and enter Burma at Tachileik, and then ride around the area for a few kilometers. Another option was to enter Myanmar riding off-pavement into the Shan State from Thailand north of Mae Hong Son, an option a Chiang Mai–based adventurist had done on several occasions in 2011 and 2012.

When I heard that barriers to entry had been cracked by the group of five claiming to be the first, my initial thought was to wonder how much it had cost to be the first, specifically what kind of money had been palmed by various government officials to grease the entry. As a number of around $1,500 per person surfaced, a second group from Malaysia entered. Their smallest motorcycle was 650cc, and their entry fee was about $1,600 per person and motorcycle.

Having ridden a yak, camel, and even an ostrich on my travels around the world, I decided it was time to try an elephant in Thailand. It didn't seem to like me and I preferred my motorcycle over letting the elephant handler set the pace and direction.

Both groups posted their tales on the Internet with photos and links. It seemed the door really had been opened, the key being the entry fee.

The particulars of their trips began to filter out and generally seemed to follow a similar trail. Permits had to be obtained well in advance with a flight plan, or route and schedule, filed with the government and approved. Government guides were required and included in the entry fee, as were hotel costs in government-approved hotels. While a third group entered and followed pretty much the earlier routes and programs, what became clear was the government of Myanmar had found a way to enter into the guided tour business. Put another way, the communist government had taken a hint from the capitalistic tour operator's world: offer packaged and guided tours and foreigners with money would pay. Neighboring China had long used a similar tactic to satisfy foreign motorcyclists' demands to drive their own motorcycles into and through limited parts of that country.

The luster of riding motorcycles over the borders into Myanmar wore off for serious adventurists like myself as we learned the guided tours were not quite the free-roaming self-guided journeys we desired. For the same amount of money, a tourist on foot could visit more of Myanmar and roam pretty freely, using airplanes, buses, minivans, and local transport. If one wanted to book a motorcycle tour inside Myanmar, that option was also available, albeit expensive and limited in geographic areas.

Clearly Myanmar was on the move. The next race will be to see if Kentucky Fried Chicken or McDonald's opens there first. Maybe I could be the first motorcyclist to fill my order riding my foreign-registered Kawasaki ZX130 into the drive-through. But $1,600 seems a bit steep for a Big Mac and bragging rights when I know I paid far less than that for the small motorcycle.

CHAPTER NINE

DOWN AND OUT
IN INDIAN COUNTRY

Karma and Cosmic

Sugar sand. The white deep stuff ate me, ending a day of primitive exploring. I would like to say the tears that dripped on Indian Route 28 that afternoon were from laughing at myself and my self-inflicted predicament, but the truth was some fell from pain.

The day started simply enough. While looking at my AAA map, I saw I had several options to reach my destination for the night: Gallup, New Mexico. I was in Holbrook, Arizona, and saw the nearly dead straight super slab of Interstate 40 would have me in Gallup within two hours. More pavement north to the Hopi Reservation and then east across two-lane Highway 264 would take me on a scenic route through Window Rock. It was a nice enough option, but one I had done at least a dozen times before.

A town named Greasewood on the Navajo Reservation drew my attention. I calculated I could drive about 50 miles on pavement and then at Greasewood take a dirt road nearly 20 miles across what showed on the map as a great empty desert to a dot called Klagetoh. There I had the choice of some more pavement and then either more dirt or sticking to Highway 191 and back onto the interstate.

As I pondered the route options, I wondered about Greasewood. "Why is the town there and why a road to there from Klagetoh? Who lives there?" And then, "How tough could 17 miles of a reservation dirt road be if it showed on a AAA road map?"

I knew if the dirt road got too tough I could always turn around and still make Gallup in time for my evening appointment. Curiosity won out over possible common sense, though, and I set off for Greasewood.

The Navajo name for the village was *Diwozhii Bil'To*, and the name on a road sign to the trading post that had been there since the early 1940s said it was Greasewood Springs, not merely Greasewood.

Down and out on the Navajo Indian Reservation, a leg-breaking spill at about 2 miles per hour. The front wheel hit a hidden rock about the size of a baseball in the deep sand, flipped over on my right leg, and snapped the bone just above the ankle. Not a good day.

As curious as I was about who and what was inside the trading post, the local Navajo shoppers and post mistress were equally curious about me and my motorcycle. My inquiries about the condition of the road out of Greasewood Springs and onto Klagetoh 17 miles away were met with, "Road's fine. Watch out for the cows and horses. Your motorcycle might spook them." Another comment was, "Don't try it in the rain. It gets real nasty. But then again, since you're on a motorcycle you might be OK."

The general consensus of my Navajo sample pool was I would be fine, as long as I didn't get "lost out there or it rains." The temperature was close to 100 degrees, no rain had been seen in days, and there was, technically, only one road, Indian Route 28. It was time to go.

Within the first mile, I saw a sign that said the road was maintained only for school buses. I thought if school buses could drive over the road, my Kawasaki KLR650 with dual-purpose tires should be able to do the same.

After that first road sign, I saw no others for the next 15 to 16 miles. There were several dirt and dust-covered roads or tracks vectoring off the main road, but none marked with much else other than a painted tire hung on a fence post likely directing people to whomever lived down that road.

The road surface varied from hardpan or packed dirt to deep sand. On the hard surfaces the trick was to weave between potholes and slow down when approaching places where the hardpan changed to soft sand. One cow tried to run with me after I stopped and took its picture. I had learned that the brain on a cow functioned in the variable mode, so never trust them standing, running, or lying down. For me, the best cow is medium well done on a plate, not alive on an open range.

This Navajo cow fit with my earlier experiences. As I started to speed up in first gear, the cow came off the mound and started to run alongside me like a dog. I accelerated, thinking I could outrun it, but then saw broken road ahead of me and slowed down. As I rolled off the throttle, the cow made a hard right turn across the road in front of me. As it ran off into the bush, I thought, "Next time I see you I hope you are on a menu."

The next miles were uneventful. I had seen no cars, trucks, buses, or motorcycles since leaving Greasewood Springs, and other than the cow the environment was mine alone to enjoy.

Two miles from Highway 191, the paved road on my map, I went down. What ate me was deep sugar sand hiding a rock the size of a baseball. I had been slowly paddling through a section of the deep white soft stuff when my front wheel hit the hidden rock, forcing the handlebars into a far right locked position. At 10 miles per hour one second I was upright, two or three seconds later I was down on my right side, face buried in the sand, right foot twisted painfully under the rear of the motorcycle, and the throttle was pegged with the engine screaming at top rpm.

Something was wrong. Lighting was shooting from my foot into every part of my body; I had felt things tear as I rolled off the motorcycle, and it took several tries before I could free my foot. Before standing up, I pushed the kill switch on the right side of the handlebar to shut off the ignition. Then I reached the key and turned off the entire system. I spit up a mouthful of sand.

At first I thought I might have broken my ankle, but despite severe pain I could move my foot and no bones felt broken. I tried to stand, but my right ankle would not support my weight.

Using the motorcycle as an aid, I was able to push myself upright. My ankle throbbed. I tried to walk off the hurt, but my vision of "manning-up" turned to tears and more than saying, "Ouch!"

I sat down on the flopped motorcycle and made a mental list of my problems: I was hurt, alone, with no cell phone on an empty road. I could wait for someone to appear for help.

That option made sense. As I sat on top of the left-side aluminum pannier, I was reminded of a woman who once told me she always carried an umbrella when she traveled. She could not pick up her BMW motorcycle, loaded or unloaded, but when it fell over in Africa, she would get out of her hot riding jacket and helmet, unpack her umbrella, and sit in its shade until help came along. As I cooked in the Arizona desert that afternoon, I wanted to kick myself for leaving my umbrella on another one of my motorcycles.

Thirty minutes went by. I had plenty of time to think about why I was where I was and the elements that had gone into the situation. I had pushed my adventure envelope no further than I felt was beyond the safe side of risk. The driving conditions were not above my skill level nor was my equipment wrong for the task chosen. A simple rock had given me a taste of bad *joss*.

After my mental debate I knew one thing: I was going to have to "cowboy up," somehow get the motorcycle upright, and move out of the hot sun. On my knees I unpacked the luggage and tossed it away from the motorcycle. My first attempt to lift the lightened motorcycle was a painful failure.

My right ankle was useless. I turned around and with my left leg doing the major work, grasping the handlebar and one of the pannier mounts, I was able to slowly work the motorcycle upward. It took several attempts, but eventually the motorcycle was upright. I leaned over the seat from the right side and levered down the kickstand, and waited for my breath to settle and vision to clear.

I met the Cosmic Adventure Rider the night before I broke my leg as we wandered Arizona around Holbrook.

Loading the gear back on the motorcycle was as painful as lifting the motorcycle. Once it was loaded, I tried to "throw my right leg over the saddle," but discovered some new pain in my rib cage and right shoulder, plus I could not lift the right leg high enough to get it over the pile of luggage. Some hopping, twisting, and sliding got my right leg over the seat and then my foot down to the right peg.

Fortunately, the KLR650 started quickly. I carefully shifted most of my weight off the left leg, let the clutch out, and one-foot paddled out of the sand. Five minutes later I was parked on the safe pavement in front of the village store at *Leeyi'to*, the Navajo word for the village of Klagetoh. I limped around to ascertain my mobility, which was severely limited.

My day of adventure riding off-pavement was over. The next miles into Gallup were slow and steady, while trying to work motion into my right foot through the swelling ankle.

That night I reflected on a short list of lessons I had learned. Most items on the list I had learned earlier and forgotten (like the umbrella). The one that was new was that I did not like the taste of sugar sand. It tastes nothing like sugar.

Several days later, x-rays proved my initial sense: I had broken my leg. With no medical insurance, I spent the next six weeks self-medicating.

It gave me time to ponder how the whole event had unfolded, that the adventure was almost cosmic. The day before the accident, I had been driving up and down the main street of Holbrook, Arizona, looking for a motel I had booked and could not find. Coming at me was a BMW R1200GS owner, also driving slow and looking at the motels on either side of the street. We turned around and made two or three more passes. I finally drove into the parking lot of a seedy motel, and he did the same.

We asked each other about inexpensive motels. I told him I had booked one but could not find it. His attempt to find it on his GPS failed. We removed our helmets, turned off our motorcycles, and introduced ourselves.

We had been fighting heavy crosswinds for the last hours, both having logged 400–500-mile days; mine started at 4 a.m., his at 6 a.m. Fourteen hours later, we independently decided to rest inside an inexpensive motel in Holbrook rather than fight more winds and sand in a local campground trying to pitch our tents for the night.

We agreed to test the price of a small mom-and pop-motel across the street. The owner told me the place I booked did not exist in the small town. The proffered price of a single room in his motel was in the acceptable zone for both my new acquaintance and me. We checked in, parked our motorcycles in front of our rooms, and agreed to walk to a nearby restaurant for dinner after washing off our road dust.

Over dinner we found much common ground: same brand and model of motorcycle helmet, same tank panniers, Gold Wing owners, and many acquaintances in common. That both of us had bagged our professional careers and opted to pursue motorcycling full-time with far less economic security was a secret we shared.

He departed well before me the next morning. I had some pressing business matters that needed serious telephone time while he wanted an early start to ride north through the Navajo Reservation toward Moab, Utah.

I left Holbrook at noon, deciding to take the small dirt road that eventually took me down. About 1:30 p.m., the heavily loaded KLR650 flopped down on my right ankle.

Two days later, as I was knocking down easy miles north of Las Vegas on Interstate 5, I saw the new acquaintance and his BMW GS headed south on a side road. The next night I sent him an e-mail saying our paths had crossed again.

He sent back an e-mail with an attached story and pictures. He too had crashed on the day we departed, also in sand, and still within the Navajo Reservation. From the time and date stamp on his attached photo, I saw he dropped his behemoth at 1:38 p.m. We had both gone down on the right side, and each of us faced the problem of muscling upright our heavily loaded motorcycles, alone and far from anywhere and anyone.

When I first saw the BMW GS rider in Holbrook, and after we removed our helmets and shook hands, I felt no déjà vu, no karmic connect. He was just another motorcyclist marked by his attire and choice of motorcycle.

Maybe his get-off or mine was the result of one of us passing onto the other some strange karma, unloading some acquired joss. Or the entire episode might have been a motorcycle adventure taste of what is on the other side. As a conservative economist, I could pass it off as a coincidence, but the odds of his X and my Y being equal were too great to be ignored.

I looked forward to keeping in contact with him, following his adventures as he pushed his adventure-seeking envelope. He had bagged nearly 38,000 miles on his BMW in 18 months, attended five off-road riding schools, and seemed committed to adventurist pursuits. Until I can wrap my head around how we met in the middle of nowhere and flopped down the next day at nearly the same time in sand, however, I am going to place the entire adventure into a cranial gray matter file called "Cosmic Motorcycle Adventurists," a file that has several other outer-limit type of adventurists in it.

CHAPTER TEN

ALASKA EXPEDITION

Far beyond the Pavement

I needed an expedition motorcycle. The plan was to travel across parts of Alaska where there were no roads, places where only snow machines, dog sleds, or a bicycle could transport people and luggage when the ground was frozen solid and covered with snow. The major difference would be timing: instead of frozen tundra and ice, the motorcycle would cross the terrain in July when much of the ground would be covered by 3-foot-deep spongy tundra. What was a hard-packed track in winter would be loose gravel, some swamp, or impassable mud wallows in July.

Some roads come to an end at a sign. I found a way around this one that kept me out of trouble.

The motorcycle needed to be light enough to be dragged through or carried over sections too deep to ride through or too soft to cross. It would also have to be powerful enough to carry camping gear, extra gas, and food to points where there would be none. Additionally, it had to be simple—one that a shade-tree mechanic like me could repair if a tire deflated or if a crash broke a clutch lever or bent a rim.

Another factor in the decision of "Which motorcycle was best for the expedition?" was the purchase price. Where the expedition was taking me, there was a possibility the motorcycle might have to be abandoned or confiscated.

The initial plan was to start in Anchorage, Alaska. From there, I would somehow get myself and my loaded motorcycle to as close to Russia as I could, and then hopefully on into Siberia after crossing the Bering Straits.

My motorcycle of choice was a 2009 Kawasaki KLX250S. I had used a KLX250 before in the jungles of Thailand and found that the 249cc engine with six-speed transmission had enough displacement

A pet caribou was ferried around Nome in the owner's pickup truck, much to the delight of locals who would pet it.

There was a wild tale involving a bar fight, wild women, and dogs behind this downed airplane in the Alaska bush outside of Nome; the purported participants declined to speak more about it.

and power to carry myself and significant gear over major highways at satisfactory speeds or through some nasty sections of slippery, narrow trails. At 277.8 pounds dry, I could unload the luggage and then drag or push it through uglier sections. I also liked the purchase price for a new model. It was not an adventure budget-buster and left some funds for the accessories I would need on the expedition.

Having been to Alaska many times since the early 1970s, I knew what to expect on the major road system there. What was an unknown were the trail or track conditions off the pavement between Anchorage and my eventual destination far to the northwest just a few miles below the Arctic Circle.

I ordered the accessories I needed to outfit the KLX250S from motorcycle adventure outfitters and had them ship the boxes to the motorcycle dealer in Anchorage, where I paid for and collected the KLX250S. When I explained where I was going, on an expedition to the Bering Sea nearly 600 miles from Anchorage as my last supply depot, each company offered some suggestions for my list of gear, including riding clothing and free advice about cold-weather riding.

The 2009 Kawasaki KLX250S was waiting along with the numerous boxes at Anchorage Kawasaki dealer. The owner had known of my planned expedition and offered some friendly advice as I signed legal papers and started to bolt and strap on parts and accessories to the KLX250S in the parking lot of his shop. "Take a sharp knife," he said. "If a polar bear comes after you, and you can run fast, maybe you can cut yourself enough to bleed out before it eats you."

The dealer also introduced me to an Alaska state trooper, who worked out of Nome. As I rode away from the motorcycle shop to break in the motorcycle, I began to wonder about his tips, thinking either he had a good sense of humor or knew something I did not about Alaska's far north.

The best-known route from Anchorage to Nome was the Iditarod Trail, famed for the annual dog-sled race in March. Leaving Anchorage on the fully loaded KLX250S to arrive at the first checkpoint about 30 minutes away was relatively easy. The four-lane paved highway was simple work for the 249cc motorcycle. When I needed a little extra zip to pass a truck or slower moving vehicle, I simply downshifted to fifth and had plenty of power.

The Iditarod race leaves the pavement in the town of Wasilla, where I stopped at the Iditarod Trail Headquarters. Here, I discovered some interesting facts about the miles ahead.

First, the 1,049 miles of the race trail to Nome was a symbolic figure. The race was really a "thousand-mile race in the 49th state," thus the number 1,049. The actually mileage was closer to 1,200, depending on which route was taken. Second, a bicycle rider had made the trip in 14 days. Third, about one foot off the gravel track into the weeds and bushes of what would be the frozen trail in March was where the Kawasaki stopped in July. Maybe another foolish motorcycle adventurer would want to spend the next two to six weeks dragging his or her motorcycle and gear over the 1,200 miles of thick weeds and brush ahead, but this one backed up to the gravel track and began mapping Plan B.

I spent the next weeks breaking in the KLX250S, testing its carrying capacity on and off pavement and checking my camping gear and the

Deep in the bush outside of Nome, Alaska, I found myself looking at the ground whenever I stopped for some of the famed gold that brought thousands of miners to the area during the days of the Gold Rush. I didn't find any gold, but I did locate some excellent roads.

I found some wild tales about life in Nome in one of its eight bars on Main Street.

This was a moneymaker—a gold dredge. It was averaging $25,000 USD per week and the owner had four of them operating. One man works atop, while the other sucks sand off the ocean floor 10 to 15 feet under water. It's cold work, but very profitable.

weather-worthiness of my riding gear. A stop in Anchorage, where they let me change the break-in oil, found me accepting their proffered advice about my expedition toward Russia: "Don't Ride Naked."

The next stops were a shopping mall and an auto-parts store where I assembled a toolkit. The toolkit that came with the Kawasaki was adequate for simple fixes, but I knew where I was going would at times put me at least 70 miles from town. Besides adding some basic tools such as a hammer and vice grips, I purchased a bicycle hand-operated air pump and tire-patch kit. Passing the ATV section in a large supermarket, I noticed two items that made sense to add to my gear. The first was a pair of snowmobile gloves that were waterproof and came nearly to my elbows. Knowing I was going to be close to the Arctic Circle, the summer riding gloves I carried with light rain covers would likely keep my hands dry, but not warm.

The second purchase was a pair of soft lever covers that easily mounted to the handlebars of not only an ATV or snow machine, but also over the levers of my motorcycle. For $15, they seemed to be a good investment against the high probability of cold rain and possibly protection in a slow speed fall.

The next decision was to go by boat versus air cargo. There were boats and barges carrying goods out of Anchorage to Nome, but they were slow and not scheduled for when I wanted to leave and arrive. An option was to ride the motorcycle north to Fairbanks or on the Dalton Highway to the Yukon River Crossing and there try to hitch a ride on a boat going down the Yukon River. That option would have been even slower than a barge out of Anchorage and likely would have left me stuck trying to find a way across the Norton Sound. In the winter, the Iditarod entrants (and the bicycle riders) could cross the Norton

Sound because it was solid ice. Not so in summer and there were few small boats making the passage.

The distance between Anchorage and Nome by air was 549 miles. A promise of a two-day air cargo delivery made this a more timely option than sitting and waiting on the banks of the Yukon River swatting mosquitoes for a week or more.

I rode the Kawasaki to the air cargo terminal at the Anchorage airport and began shopping for the best deal. The range in prices by various air cargo companies varied, depending upon when I wanted the motorcycle in Nome. The price of $750, uncrated, would deliver it to Nome in a promised day; $500 uncrated would get it there on a less expensive carrier but with no promise that it would be there anytime soon. The $750 offer seemed best, especially if I had to wait a week.

The air carrier I selected changed rules about halfway through the packing process. Some backroom bureaucrat concluded the motorcycle had to be shipped as two units not as one, as I had previously been told. The bureaucrat wanted all the bags (tank bag, fender bag, headlight pod bag, saddlebag, windscreen, and luggage) stripped off and shipped in a separate box. I hassled some lackey while the unknown bureaucrat hid in his or her office and issued interpretations of rules, one of the wildest being saddlebags on motorcycles were not fixed items and thus had to be removed.

The other hassle was the airline counter person, who wanted me to pay a freight forwarding company located across town to fill out the one page form I had already correctly completed for Dangerous Goods. This process would likely take half a day and cost up to $150, not counting taxi fares and possibly an additional night in a motel in Anchorage at $110 for the least expensive room near the airport.

Eventually the bureaucrat either went out for lunch or home for the day and the counter person decided the properly presented Dangerous Goods form I supplied would suffice. The motorcycle was stripped of all accessories, which were boxed and shipped separately. With the battery disconnected and gas tank drained, the motorcycle was weighed, then measured for overall space displacement, and my credit card was whacked with the promise my motorcycle would be waiting for me the next day when I arrived in Nome.

Two days later the motorcycle arrived and I reassembled it at the air cargo bay in Nome. A friendly worker there volunteered a liter of gas and my expedition began. The only good part of the air cargo experience, other than meeting some nice workers in Nome and Anchorage, was a telephone call from one employee telling me that the bureaucrat had been incorrect: saddlebags were considered an integral part of the motorcycle, and if I wanted to ship the motorcycle back to Anchorage using their company, I would not have to remove them.

At the first gas station I stopped at in Nome, the cashier asked, "What kind of motorcycle is that?"

"It's a Kawasaki," I said.

"Don't see many of those up here, not that kind."

"Have you ever seen any?" I asked.

He scratched his beard and then answered, "Nope. We've got a couple of Harley-Davidsons, some Yamahas, and a Honda or two. Where're you going with that Kawasaki?"

"I'm going to see if I can get out to Council, maybe Taylor, then up to Teller, and across to Russia from there."

He laughed and said, "You won't see the Harleys on that route. Heck, even the dog sleds in the Iditarod stop here in Nome. You're headed where few people go unless they have to."

My expedition out of Nome was looking up. I'd be going where loud pipes were not trying to save lives and I possibly had dealt with the last bureaucrat for a few miles.

"There's no place like Nome" says the Nome Convention and Visitors Bureau. After five rides around the globe and 1 million miles, I had to admit in the first hour the town was far different from any other I had passed through. The mileage post on Main Street read

In Nome I was far from most places, but Siberia was only 164 miles across the water.

166

Summer in Nome isn't warm, but I'll take it over winter's freezing snow and wind.

The Dexter Bar sits about 12 miles outside of Nome. It opens at 2 a.m. and closes at 5 a.m. The owner's old BMW sat behind it, the only BMW in Nome.

that Denver was 3,402 miles southeast and Siberia was 164 miles west across the Bering Sea that lapped the shore only a few yards away. I knew I was not in Kansas anymore.

My first stop was the visitors bureau to inquire about cheap sleeping. The screaming green Kawasaki KLX250S, yelling High-Viz Darien jacket from Aerostich, and yellow Nolan motorcycle helmet made me a highly visible target on Main Street in the town with a population of less than 4,000. Before I had taken off my helmet, an attractive and energetic reporter from the *Nome Nugget* newspaper headquartered across the street ran out the door and over to my parked motorcycle where she asked, "Hi. Who are you and what are you doing here, and what kind of motorcycle is that?"

The old lone-wolf traveler that I am, I have learned that a pretty face asking pointed questions can lead down several paths, some good, others to a disaster. My cautious response was, "I'm trying to get to Russia on the cheap from up north at Teller."

She looked my motorcycle over and then at me again, then said, "I work for the *Nome Nugget*, Alaska's oldest newspaper. Can I take your picture and interview you for an article?"

The path I chose to follow this time was a good one. I first spent a profitable half hour in the visitors bureau finding a reasonably inexpensive room for the night versus sleeping on the beach for free in the wind and rain. Walking across the street, I saw the portable finish line for the Iditarod that the organizers pull across Main Street in early March. As I took a photo of the sign on skids, I tried to imagine how cold it would be in early March as the entrants mushed into Nome after 1,200 miles of the torturous event from Anchorage. "Cold enough to freeze your nose hairs!" was what I had been told at the visitors bureau. I decided then that while Nome looked like a friendly city, one that did not have a stoplight, and I had already met one pretty lady, it was not where I wanted to be on my motorcycle other than when I was there, the end of June, their "high season" with a normal high of 58.6 degrees and low of 46.

The *Nome Nugget* publisher was working at the front desk when I entered. When I asked about circulation and some history, she proudly told me it was the only newspaper for more than 500 hundred miles in any direction and published every day, except for Monday, Tuesday, Wednesday, Friday, Saturday, and Sunday.

The interview appeared with a photo on Thursday, so my 15 minutes of fame in the Nome area lasted for a week. In the interview, I said I was interested in meeting people and asked that people stop and talk to me, which they often did after reading the article and seeing me.

After my interview, I took several photographs of where the famous Dexter saloon used to be located, the ground on which now stands Nome City Hall. When Wyatt Earp (yes, the one from Tucson and the OK Corral) owned the Dexter in 1897, it was the only two-story building in town. This was during the Alaska Gold Rush, and the town swelled to more than 28,000. Earp returned to the States in 1901 with reportedly $80,000, and none of that he had to dig out of the ground or sift off the beach. One could say he had mined the miners.

While I was taking photographs of the street, the bartender of the Board of Trade Saloon came out and took a few photographs of my parked Kawasaki and then of me taking photographs of the saloon. The Board of Trade Saloon was one of eight saloons in town.

This summer house, also known as a camp, was one of many squatter sites outside Nome that afforded residents the ability to enjoy being away from the city.

Shed caribou antlers made for some Alaska bush "bling" for my motorcycle.

I camped where I could in Nome, praying that bears would keep their distance.

It was also the oldest, built in 1900, and had printed on the front "Headquarters for the Sin City of Nome."

The Board of Trade was not only a saloon, but also housed an ivory and artifact shop, a pull-tab room, and a large bingo hall upstairs with free food on bingo nights. The friendly bartender told me the owner had seen me walking on the street and wanted to meet me.

When I started to lock the Kawasaki, the bartender laughed and told me no one would steal it. "Where would they hide it?" he asked. "And with that color, they couldn't ride it, if they did take it, without the police immediately spotting it. Don't worry, but I'd lock it at night; someone might want to take it for a test ride."

The proprietor proved to be a most likeable person, with many stories and wild tales of Nome having lived there more than 50 years. He had come to Nome from Arkansas and started working as a house painter. After 50 successful years, he hired house painters to paint some of the numerous houses and apartments that his son managed around Nome.

He asked the bartender to give me a tour of the facilities. After we finished the walkthrough of the buildings, the owner gave me an ivory Billiken for good luck, carved in the image of a small smiling person. "If you are going to be riding that motorcycle and hanging around here, you'll need the luck to keep from getting run over by drivers, bears, or caribou," he said. "Keep an eye out for the women too. Rub the Billiken belly for luck."

Before I left I stopped in the bar, drank a soda, and chatted with the bartender who gave me some of his artwork, comics that he created on his computer. As I was leaving, he reached into a large glass jar behind the bar and scooped out a handful of multicolored packets that he handed to me and said, "You can use those if you're hanging around here for a few days." Two days later, when I fished one out of my pocket to snack on while driving to Council, thinking it was wrapped candy, I discovered they were flavored condoms. I had not been in town two hours and already discovered most of the people were not only friendly but had a good sense of humor. The bar owner had me rubbing the belly of the Billiken for luck and the bartender was outfitting me with condoms.

Maps and printed material boasted more than 350 miles of a road system in, around, and out of the Nome area. These included several miles of pavement, more miles of gravel roads, and then some tracks and trails. The Kawasaki had been set up for whatever I thought the

Some serious off-road riding found me a moose antler—more bling for my motorcycle!

The solitude of Alaska was well worth the risk of the adventure. Alaska does not get much better than the area outside Nome. I was alone in the camping area and only shared the lake with the birds and a few salmon.

My dinner for the night was usually coffee, canned spaghetti, and some dried beef jerky.

area could throw at me, so I decided to ride every mile of road, track, trail, and beach I could before my schedule became tight and I had to reach Teller, there hopefully finding a way to cross the Bering Straits to Siberia. I also wanted to learn about the motorcycling community (if there was one) 141 miles below the Arctic Circle.

For the next 10 days I used Nome as a base, riding out to the ends of the three main roads, and then poking my way back while exploring any trail or track I saw. Everything I needed I carried with me, from extra gasoline, to food, tent, and sleeping bag. I also packed all spare parts I thought I might need, such as inner tubes and master link for the chain. I knew if I broke down in the bush, it could be 80 to 90 miles from Nome, well off the main road, and a long walk out.

In Alaska, camping was free and quiet, and I was alone except for the hungry, buzzing mosquitoes.

I had to carry spare gas because my Kawasaki KLX250S had only a 2-gallon gas tank, and that wasn't enough to carry me to out of Nome and then make it back to the city again. The only person I saw for miles was my reflection in the mirrors.

A remote hot springs offered the soaker a fine view of the mountains.

I planned to return to Nome every two or three days, buy more food and gas, and then go back out into the bush. After two days in Nome "discovering" the town and making friends, I left for my first target, the small village of Council, 57 miles southeast of Nome. While it is described as an abandoned village, there are numerous summer homes with part-time residents. With the summer fishermen and birders, the population sometimes reached 50 to 100 on a busy weekend. In the late 1890s, before the rush to Nome, there were as many as 15,000 residents in this now sleepy village.

The first leg for 30 miles was littered with dead gold-mining equipment, trucks, cars, snow machines, ATVs, and squatters' summerhouses along the beach. I soon learned that nothing is thrown away in this remote part of Alaska. If a truck died, it was not sent to the crusher 1,000 miles away. It was sold for parts to another resident or kept for possible resurrection. The same applied to ATVs, snow machines, and even airplanes. The numerous abandoned giant gold dredges that had chewed their way through the tundra were in stark contrast to the lush green scrub brush all around.

That winter, much of the early section of the road from Nome to Council was hardpan. There was a roadhouse (bar and restaurant) where I stopped for my last cooked meal. Inside were hundreds of photos on the walls of famous and not-so-famous racers. The roadhouse during the race was the final checkpoint before the last dash into Nome. During the race, several hundred dogs, racers, and fans would be milling in and around it. On my stop in June, I was the only person inside besides the lady who was the cook and barkeeper and her two children.

When the road turned inland at what was once Dickson and away from the Norton Sound, I was surprised to see three dead steam train engines and several flatbed cars slowly sinking into the mud where they had stopped more than 80 years earlier.

The rest of the road to Council was loose gravel and hardpan over barren hills and through some valleys. Streams had good bridges over them until the road ended at the Niukluk River. Across the river were an airstrip and the small village of Council. The river was wide but in late June only about 2 to 3 feet deep at the deepest point. In the winter it would be frozen and easily crossable, but in June it would be a submarine test for any motorcycle or ATV that had an air intake below the 3-foot level. Being an old global traveler has some advantages, though, one knowing that crossing deep streams 57 miles from the nearest town and ending up on a riverbank trying to dry out a hydro-locked motor and wet electrics while bears feed on salmon nearby was not an adventure I needed to experience again. I waited until a Council resident arrived from Nome in a four-wheel-drive pickup and let him ferry me across the water.

While I was interested in the town of Council and the area around it, what piqued my adventure lust was the dotted line on the map that was described as a "winter trail" following the Ophir Creek that went northeast out of Council. In the summer the locals told me I could get as far as 17 miles up the road before it became impassable (mud) and my likelihood of seeing bear or moose would be quite high. While I saw no bear, I did see a dead Honda motorcycle with bullet holes through the gas tank and found half a moose antler. I also found thick clouds of mosquitoes, a light rain all night, and cold sleeping on the ground.

The next night I was back in Nome, sleeping indoors, dry and away from the bugs. I bought gas and provisions for the next expedition out to the end of the Taylor Highway to Serpentine Hot Springs, or as far as I could ride.

While I was in Nome, a KTM rider stopped next to my Kawasaki KLX and asked what the selling price would be if I were to sell it. I told him what I would ask, but added that I wanted to ride the Taylor Highway first, and then up to Teller. He asked if I would like company on the Taylor Highway for the ride toward Kougarok, where his family owned a summerhouse. He had a friend with a Honda 650XR who could go with us and we would make an afternoon adventure. He painted a fun picture of the secrets he knew of the road, so I decided to make it a trio and let the locals drag me along.

When I asked him what would be interesting for my Nome evening, he said there were the bars (which I had already seen once and at $5 for a beer, once was enough). I told him I would pass. He then suggested the small movie theater, which I sloughed off thinking I did not come to Nome to go to the movies. Finally he said, "Given

Camping at Teller, Alaska, was free, and my only visitors during the night were seagulls scrounging for food.

In the small village at the end of one road, I made friends with several of the local tribal members. When I asked what they did in the winter, they said, "Not much."

This was the only motorcycle I found in the village of Teller, Alaska.

what you have seen around the world, maybe you'd find the Dexter Roadhouse interesting."

"What and where is it?" I asked.

It was a saloon about 15 minutes from Nome, outside the city limits, he said. It opened after the saloons in town closed at 2 a.m. or 3 a.m. "Who goes out there at 2 or 3 in the morning?" I asked.

He laughed, and then said, "Some local people I think you would find very interesting, and the owner rides an old BMW motorcycle."

That night I woke up when the saloon below my sleeping room closed at 2 a.m. and the swillers and spillers stumbled up the stairs and down the hall to their sleeping rooms. I dressed in my warmest clothes and rode over the hill in a cold fog to have a soda at 3 a.m. in the Dexter Roadhouse. My new KTM friend was right; it was an interesting group, some of which were intent on keeping their festivities going that had started earlier in Nome. The owner and I traded BMW R60 tales and tips on where to get parts until 4 a.m., when I had consumed enough cola and coffee to keep me awake for the rest of the night. From my room in Nome at 5:30 a.m., I could see and hear some of the people I had met earlier at the Dexter Roadhouse coming back to their Nome starting points.

As I fell asleep at 6 a.m., going over my mental checklist for things I needed to do before heading toward Kougarok and then the Serpentine Hot Springs, the one statement that kept going through my head was, "There's no place like Nome." I spent nearly two weeks driving the KLX250S over every possible piece of ground I could cover in, around, and out of Nome, bagging nearly 1,000 miles. Someday I would like to return and re-ride my Alaska expedition.

CHAPTER ELEVEN

CAMBODIA JUNGLE RUN

No Stranger to Danger

The rule I had made for myself when traveling in and out of third-world countries was never to use a motorcycle I could not afford to lose or leave behind—whether the separation was from a crash, theft, confiscation by crooked authorities, or a serious mechanical breakdown. This rule was dubbed the Marginal Propensity to Foolishly Incur Significant Economic Loss Due to Unnecessary Ego Feeds.

This pig was on the way to market, kicking and squealing as if it knew what was coming.

Over my 40 years of roaming the globe, I had seen fellow motorcycle travelers spend huge sums of money to retrieve, or attempt to retrieve, broken or crashed motorcycles, often spending amounts that far exceeded the value of the motorcycle. One example was a fellow traveler who needed a new engine for his broken motorcycle while in Argentina, where none of the models were ever imported or sold. Importing a replacement engine cost two to three times the purchase price of a used one in good condition from the United States due to shipping costs and extremely high Argentine import taxes.

Thinking he could circumvent the air-freight costs and customs taxes, he purchased a used engine off the Internet, then a round-trip airline ticket to fly to the United States and return carrying the disassembled engine parts he needed as personal luggage. After adding up the costs of the engine, airline ticket, taxis, hotels, and shop time in Argentina for damaged engine removal, disassembly, reassembly and reinstallation, he spent twice the worth of the dead motorcycle.

Fried spider for a snack? I tried it once. It crunched like a fried eyeball, which I also tried once.

Another motorcycle traveler had secured government permission to ride his expensive motorcycle into Vietnam, a country known for strictly applied rules about bringing in large displacement motorcycles (more than 175cc). With his government-issued letter of permission to enter, he happily piloted his $20,000 motorcycle through the country where most motorcycles cost in the range of $600 to $2,500. When he tried to exit the country, the border guards allowed him to depart but not his motorcycle. They noted that while his government-issued letter gave permission to enter the country with his motorcycle, nowhere in it did it authorize him to leave the country with it. After confiscating his motorcycle, he was sent on his way by foot into Laos, the next country. After a considerable amount of time and money, including three return flights from his country of origin, the traveler was eventually able to secure the release of his motorcycle from halfway around the world and fly it home at a cost that far surpassed the bike's value.

I did not want to use a large motorcycle (600cc) for an expedition into Cambodia from Thailand. Instead, I chose my $750, 200cc 1989 Kawasaki KMX. Neither the 600cc model nor the 200cc KMX had ever been imported to either country, so if either broke or quit running I would be faced with either a long wait and tiresome import requirements for parts, or I might have to abandon one or the other. The KMX was the smaller loss, and one that I could afford.

A small load being towed to market. Thankfully, I didn't have as much gear as these guys.

My Cambodian Jungle Runner, all 200cc of it. From Thailand to Cambodia and back, it proved that a big-displacement motorcycle wasn't necessary for an extreme adventure.

I also took into consideration some geographic areas where I would be traveling once inside Cambodia where roads or local residents might not be friendly toward a foreigner on an expensive big motorcycle. Simply put, being a foreigner piloting an obviously expensive motorcycle equated to "Here I am, some rich guy traveling alone, in your country where this motorcycle costs 100 times your per capita income."

I spent two weeks readying the KMX for the expedition. I installed new inner tubes in the tires and devised a carrying system for clothes, tools, cameras, and spare parts. I installed a new battery, oiled the chain, and checked all the cables.

Before leaving my base in Chiang Mai, Thailand, I made several small test rides through town. On the eve of the planned departure, the prepped Kawasaki KMX 200 was on a final shakedown run with luggage strapped on to test the motorcycle's suspension. A stop at a local travel agency where I knew the owner found her looking at it and describing it to me as "sexy."

That was a new twist, an interesting description. To get a second opinion, I parked the motorcycle on a street well known for the small bars staffed by prostitutes. Outside the first bar, a flock of the night doves swarmed around it, some wanting to sit on it, others asking me to take them for a ride.

I asked one of the ladies it if she thought it was sexy. Her name was Pee. "Yes, sexy, very sexy," she answered. "You handsome man. Where you from? What your name?"

In my broken Thai, I answered, "My motorcycle is from Japan, the only one in Thailand. Me, I am from an Indian reservation in Montana, the only Big Indian Boom-Boom in Thailand. Do you want to go for a ride?"

She laughed, then answered, "I work now, you pay my bar fine?"

Laughing with her, I replied, "I no pay your bar fine. You pay bar fine for me."

The whole covey of doves was now laughing. I saw that Pee was confused though. I tried to help her understand what I was proposing. I told her the motorcycle had been meticulously prepared over the previous weeks for a long and arduous expedition into the jungles along the Thai and Cambodia borders. I carefully explained that if she wanted to go for a short ride for a little fun, she would have to pay for the pleasure, starting with 400 Baht ($25), the same as the bar fine would be for me to take her out of the bar for a short time. I tried to help her understand that like her rice canoe, there were only so many times or kilometers the unit could be used before it became worn out, that prepared as it was, it was now in its prime.

She understood the rice canoe analogy as all working professionals understand the letters A, T, and M. A deal was finally negotiated, and the KMX had the first of its many adventures, although it was more like a warmup lap than a lengthy race. As the KMX was ridden out of the urban concrete jungle, it was followed by jealous cries from the tittering birds left standing on the sidewalk outside the bar.

The first hours of riding the next morning were uneventful, giving me time to reflect on the send-off I had received the night before. Fully loaded, the two-stroke Kawasaki was happy at 90 kilometers per hour, ripping along at 6,000–7,000 rpm. Every 80 kilometers I would have to start looking for petrol because of the small 2-gallon gas tank. The pit stop would give me a nice break about once an hour. With six gears I was able to maintain my speed up hills by downshifting to lower gears, and if I wanted to pass a truck or slower moving vehicle, I could kick it down a cog and zip around. The 200cc engine was performing flawlessly.

An hour after a greasy lunch at a gas stop, my gut started to burble. My personal chugging exhaust chute told me things in my lower intestine needed to be handled before I could reach the next pit stop. A tentative eruption from my bottom end caused me to pull off the road, barely get the side stand down, and dash for the trees and surrounding bushes.

I heard the Kawasaki fall over as I ran away, but I had more pressing concerns. As I ran into the jungle, I pulled off my gloves, helmet, and tried to get out of my riding armor, and get the suspenders

A portable Coke-Cola stand in Cambodia.

on my riding pants down. The twitches of my sphincter were seconds apart as I stumbled behind a tree, dropped my pants, and squatted. I let go with a blast and groaned with relief, a human feeling of physical satisfaction often held above all others.

In my gentle repose, I felt something moving under my right boot. I looked down and saw my foot was on top of a snake that was trying to wiggle out from underneath. I had pushed the snake's head into the soft jungle mat. In my rush to clear my colon, I had squatted in the first serviceable site, well within range of a very mad Siamese or king cobra, now inches from my exposed manhood and baby soft back end.

A bite from one of these snakes can kill an elephant. I thought about doing the tough-guy thing, such as slowing lifting my foot, reaching down quickly, and grabbing the cobra behind the head and then throwing it as far as I could.

Another motorcycle hitches a ride to the next town in the back of a minivan. This was not an unusual sight in Cambodia. Motorcycles were often toted around on top of taxis and buses.

Sometimes things get grim. That husk of a building on the left was what some families called home, while the town dump sits across the street.

I chose, however, the most unmanly thing imaginable: I screamed and jumped away as far as I could. There was nothing pretty about my getaway. I landed headfirst and my pants were still below my knees. Rolling forward two or three times through the bushes while wildly thrashing, I tried to get as far away as I could before worrying about what might make me a eunuch or using toilet paper.

I finally stopped and stood, pulled my pants up, and quickly hobbled back to the downed motorcycle, not looking back to see where the snake was, just wanting to be out of the jungle, his turf, and back on the pavement, my turf.

After using a handful of cleansing wipes I had stored in my tank bag, I wiped and dressed. Picking up the motorcycle was the next chore. When I did, I noticed there was no return spring pressure against the throttle. The plastic coupling to the carburetor and the

It was cheaper to use the ferryboat than to pay the toll on the newly completed bridge nearby.

oil injector had been jammed against the expansion chamber and melted. I was screwed.

It was nearly dark when I tried to connect the cables. The light disappeared, and I tried working while using my flashlight, but nothing I cobbled together was good enough. Depressed, with no water and a pissed-off snake somewhere nearby, I decided to push the bike to an abandoned *sala* (bamboo rest stop and shop area) across the road and sleep there for the night, try to think through a fix for the cable, and deal with it at first light. At least I would be off the ground a foot or two, and I hoped, above all animals that slithered.

I slept in my clothes, wearing my helmet and gloves. It was cool where I was, somewhere in the mountains. Sleep was elusive because I kept thinking about the snake and whether it would cross the road

An afternoon rain made this dirt road almost impassable. Two years later the road had been paved, taking much of the adventure out of it.

When the mud built up like this, I felt more like I was skiing than driving a motorcycle.

looking for me or if it had friends on my side of the road. Several times I heard animals moving through the bushes, but when I turned on my flashlight, I could see nothing and things would quiet down.

Around 2 a.m. I awoke when I heard the motorcycle fall over. I turned on my flashlight and saw 10 to 15 pairs of eyes looking at me from around the downed vehicle. It had been pushed over by a group of monkeys, white-handed gibbons. They were trying to tear open the tank bag where I had left some uneaten cookies and chips that I had planned to eat for breakfast.

I yelled and ran at the monkeys. They scattered, and then as I got closer to the motorcycle they started to circle me. They tried to grab me, hissing and yapping, and I kicked back. Next we were in a heated battle, them darting in and out of my reach as I tried to throttle them with my weary boots. They were quick little bastards, ducking in and out, sometimes yanking at parts on the motorcycle, other times snatching at my pants. I finally connected with one of the slower ones and booted it about 10 meters away. As it flew, it howled and screeched in rage, but finally stayed where it landed. The others backed away. I ran at them again and yelled; it was a standoff. Finally, the group melted into the bush and I was alone.

I was self-sufficient when traveling in Cambodia. The 25-year-old motorcycle sometimes needed a mechanic, and I was the guy for the job.

My Cambodia adventure was fun, as long as my motorcycle was running.

The motorcycle had suffered some damage. The windscreen was cracked and the gas line had been ripped off and was nowhere to be found. In the morning, I decided to use the breather hose off the battery to replace the missing gas line, glue the crack in the windscreen, and fashion a connector for the throttle cable out of a piece of a soda can. I was back on the road by 8 a.m., but it had been an ugly 15 hours at that toilet stop. As I rode, I remembered what Prince Charles once said when asked what he had learned in his many travels: "Always use a toilet when you see one." Had I done that at my last gas stop I would have never met the snake and the clan of nasty monkeys.

As I rode toward Cambodia, I thought the next three weeks were going to be more of a gauntlet ride through the jungles than a mild adventure, if the first night of the road was any indication of what was ahead. It was nothing like a sexy expedition.

CHAPTER TWELVE

SOLO NO MORE

Circumnavigating the Globe with a Passenger

Two-up on a single motorcycle changed the dynamics of a global circumnavigation beyond my expectations. Of all the rides around the world I had done, carrying a passenger was the toughest.

Carol and Ken Duval, from Australia, shared some of their experiences riding around the world two-up when we met in Kathmandu, Nepal.

"It must be hard to ride a motorcycle around the world. What do you do after you have ridden around it four times?"

A 61-year-old woman who had never been on a motorcycle before I met her was asking me these questions. Confident after years of experience, "It's not so hard," I told her, "when I made my first global loop, there were less than 100 of us who had done one. Today, with the Internet and ease of getting across water, there are probably 200 riders out there right now claiming to be riding around the world. All you really need is time and money. I am done with all that now, retired. I will probably do what others have done—write a book—maybe give some talks or multimedia shows, bask in what some think is glory."

"Would you do it again?"

My answer was quick. "No. I do not have the money and I need some time to make some more. My next project is to ride a motorcycle around the moon, and I figure that is going to cost me a bit more than any of my last four rides."

Then she hooked me with her next question. "Would you take me around the world, on the back of a motorcycle, before you ride around the moon?"

On our test ride, I piloted a 2001 Kawasaki KLR650 with Donna-Rae on the back to some far reaches in Alaska. This is the most northwesterly point we could drive on the North American continent.

10   ▶10A

I looked at her, thinking, "Is she crazy? She must be. She does not know the difference between a cam chain or drive chain, likes the comforts of fine food and four star hotels, and has Parkinson's disease with a capital P. She cannot even close a chinstrap on a motorcycle helmet. How would I manage her around the world on the back of a motorcycle? Strap ourselves together with bungee cords?"

My interest was piqued though. Just how much of a challenge would it be? I had hooked up with some lady travelers before. Almost always I found their riding lifestyles unlike mine, and I often ended up foolishly pandering to them like a normal junkyard dog does when he gets through the fence.

Her name was Donna-Rae, and we spent hours talking about how I travel, hunt roads, and manage my life on the road. She seemed more excited as I tried to make a global ride sound more difficult. In the end we struck a deal: if we planned a trip around the world, tagging the farthest points north and south, we could ride on the continents, and if we could get it done in less than a year, and if we could do it on a medium budget, and if we could do it in legs or sections, with time off for me to catch up on writing assignments—and if her Parkinson's did not get too bad—maybe we could do it.

There were a lot of other "ifs," but the biggest was, "We'll do the tagging of Ushuaia, Argentina, the farthest point south on the South American continent, 'if' you can survive the first leg, tagging Deadhorse, Alaska, the farthest point north we can ride on the North American continent."

In the back of my mind were a couple of other nagging "ifs." The first was, "If you and I can survive each other." I felt like my long-lived

After reaching Deadhorse, Donna-Rae wanted to make sure she could go no farther north. Here she is as close to the Arctic Ocean as she wanted to get on the northernmost point we could ride on the continent.

On the Dalton Highway headed south, we stopped to look back north on some of the gravel and ugly road we had encountered earlier in the morning.

lone-wolf lifestyle would become gelded if I took on the responsibility of someone else, especially a woman, on the back of my bike. I was also thinking, "This adventure could end up more like being castrated before turning me loose in the Playboy Mansion while Hef was away."

I also had a plan. I did not mind making another ride to Alaska and Prudhoe Bay. The run up North America's farthest northern road can sometimes make hardened riders turn around and go home with their tails between their legs. That road, the Dalton Highway, is one of my favorite roads in the world, though, because it can be tough, dangerous, and it changes daily. It's always interesting. I also wanted to get my 'round-the-world Kawasaki KLR650 out of retirement. It had been resting for nearly two years after finishing a 20,000-mile ride, and I wanted to see how well it would do with two of us on it. Here, I thought, was an opportunity to have someone share some of my costs up to Deadhorse and back, and it would only take me a month of time. I may have also been thinking that if I made the ride as I usually do—a little bit on the rougher side with some off-road riding mixed in—my passenger would see how hard a 'round-the-world ride like I make them might be, and we could call the rest of the trip quits.

I told her, "OK, we'll do it. Up and back. We'll see everything we're likely to see down through South America and across the Andes to Ushuaia. If you can manage Deadhorse, we will start making plans for the second leg." Secretly I thought I could beat her up enough that she would be glad to halt what she thought would be her ultimate journey, thus not embarrassing both of us if I failed.

Our first real "test days" were out of Anchorage with a small group from the American Motorcyclist Association and Kawasaki, five fun guys who were in the area for a week. They let us tag along to Homer. Half the day was in the rain, so my passenger got wet. Then once we left the AMA team at their hotel, she and I headed to the Homer Spit, where we put our tent up in the rain. We had discussed camping on our trip around the world, which I was against because of the space needed for all our gear. Our first night, sleeping on the wet rocks and making her a "Spit Rat," pounded one nail in the camping coffin. In Homer, Alaska, the sand spit out into the ocean in Homer is called the Homer Spit, and the workers who camp out there for the summer, because housing is too expensive in town, are called Spit Rats.

When we awoke at 4 a.m., it was still raining. She had been wet most of the night from two or three trips to the toilet, a nocturnal adventure caused by her medication. A budget breakfast at McDonald's warmed her up some, but seeing the five hotel guys all fresh and dry after their pampered night between the sheets, she cooled back down. A couple of morning hours of riding in the rain added some more chills. When we arrived back in Anchorage, she was ready for a hot shower and warm restaurant food.

Before leaving for Deadhorse, Donna-Rae wanted to spend a few days being a tourist in Anchorage while I went off and played with the AMA/Kawasaki team, to which I agreed. She did her shopping and looked for whales out of Seward on a train and boat trip, while I did photo and film work with the five other guys. It was the first trip to Alaska for several of them, so for me great fun to see the wilds of the North through their eyes.

We did some riding, which would have been difficult had my passenger been on the back, and I think she would not have had fun because I would have undoubtedly dropped her on the ground a few

times. And like boys do when riding, we did some bonding, genitalia scratching, and chest-thumping after conquering a few fun off-road tracks. We also saw several places I had missed on previous rides into Alaska, adding to my knowledge of motorcycling in this huge state. After more than 20 visits, I had managed to miss what they saw on their first ride. With less than a 20 percent chance of seeing Mount McKinley on any day because of clouds, we managed to pass it on a day when the sky was crystal clear. I could not have made a more perfect day for them, and hoped they knew how lucky they were.

When I returned to Anchorage, I collected my passenger and we tagged Deadhorse, then logged many more miles before I dropped her off back at her home in Colorado. As we parted she asked, "When do we leave for South America?" I couldn't believe it; I had failed in beating her dream out of her. A week later we met for lunch and mapped out our time and costs for South America.

With Mount McKinley in the background, we headed to Fairbanks, where we decided if we could tackle the Dalton Highway to Deadhorse, Alaska. McKinley only shows itself this clearly about 20 percent of the year.

Colombia

Colombia has a reputation for danger. If I believed all the tall tales about Colombia, however, I would huddle in a corner of my basement, quivering, while watching the country roll by on the Discovery

We often explored some of the villages we passed, some well away from good roads.

Channel. I wanted to surprise Miguel Giesener, a friend I had made on my ride through Colombia in 1997.

On that earlier ride, my BMW had broken and the Giesener family from Cali had put me up in their daughter's room for a week while I waited for parts to be flown in from the United States. While waiting, Miguel introduced me to a wide number of his motorcycling friends, and I found all of them to be warm and friendly. My plan for the trip with my passenger on the back was to show up on his doorstep on Christmas Eve unannounced with a few presents in thanks for his hospitality in 1997.

If Miguel's jaw could have dropped any lower when he saw me it would have hit his belt buckle. I was the last person he expected to see Christmas Eve with an armload of presents spouting "*Feliz Navidad.*" Miguel insisted my passenger, Donna-Rae, and I spend the evening with his family and friends, where dancing followed their traditional Christmas meal. Miguel's English is about as good as my Spanish, so it took him and I several hours to trade seven years of news. I learned his daughters had grown to be wives and mothers living in the United States. Sadly, Miguel told me my lady friend from 1997 had been shot and killed in her hair salon while cutting a customer's hair. The male customer was the target of a contract killing and the assassins decided to shoot the witness too. She left two small children and an empty hole in my warm memories of that earlier visit.

On Christmas Day, Donna-Rae and I went to the horse parade that takes place in Cali, where mostly rich horse people show off their best horses. The sidewalks were packed and I was the mark for a pickpocket who got my wallet. Despite four rides around the world and hundreds of other crowded places such as Times Square on New Year's Eve or Mardi Gras in New Orleans, this was the first time I had my wallet clipped. What could have been a disaster turned out to be a $10 lesson on following my instincts. Before leaving our room that morning, I had carefully gone through my wallet and removed nearly everything of value. I moved my passport to a secret pocket sewn on the inside of my Levi pants leg. I left the $400 cash I was carrying with several credit cards hidden in my riding clothes, which were thrown in the corner of the hotel room. What the dipper got when he went through my wallet were some business cards, one credit card, some papers with Cali telephone numbers written on them, and a $10 bill.

I realized immediately when my wallet was taken. I had it in my front pants pocket and I felt the dip, but by the time it registered in my mind what it was, the thief had melted into the shoulder-to-shoulder crowd we were wedging through. A quick trip back to the hotel for the telephone numbers for VISA and a long-distance

Riding down the west coast of South America we found ourselves reflecting on how far we had come from Deadhorse, Alaska, and the snow we encountered there.

Sand and the overloaded motorcycle did not make for fun adventure riding. I gave up, turned around, and drove back to the pavement.

telephone call from a phone booth had the credit card killed in two hours. As most of the stores were closed because it was Christmas Day, I doubted the thief would have been able to charge much but was relieved to hear the VISA representative tell me that nothing had.

The next day, Miguel wanted us to take his big BMW R100 GSPD motorcycle while he and his wife rode his BMW R60 for a ride in the country. Before we left, he received a telephone call from someone who had found my wallet lying on the sidewalk. They found Miguel's telephone number inside and my cards, and returned the wallet to me that morning. All that was missing was the $10. Even the small "Good Luck" Buddha given to me by a friend was still inside. My lesson was to keep listening to that little voice that sometimes whispers into my gray matter to do things that seem unreasonable at the time, such as leaving my money and credit cards in a hotel room that could easily be searched by hotel personnel while I am out. That little voice has whispered many odd things to me in life and I have always followed what I heard. I will try to keep listening to it.

Working our way south from Colombia, we found ourselves spending several days as guests of Ricardo Rocco Paz in Quito, Ecuador. Ricardo had stayed at my house the summer before, and we both own Kawasaki KLR motorcycles. He made a thorough inspection of our Honda GL 650 Silverwing and said he thought it was a smart choice for where we were planning to ride.

I chose the Silverwing because it had low mileage and few scratches. It also had a reputation of being a solid motorcycle and fell in one of what are called "Dr. G's Rules for Riding in Third World Countries": never take a motorcycle you cannot afford to lose to a thief, crash, or

In Patagonia, we stopped to help this German rider repair his flat tire. Some days later we heard that after we left him he had a heart attack, ending his attempt to reach the bottom of South America. When I looked for him on the return trip north, I was told he had been flown back to Germany.

Oops! My bike fell down.

confiscation by authorities. I call this one our $1,500 special because that is what I had invested in it before preparing it for the trip. The money we saved over buying some new $15,000–20,000 motorcycle for this ride should get us quite a ways around the earth.

Peru took longer than I had expected to get through. Part of the delay was due to work I had to do for a publisher, part due to a reoccurring bout from malaria I had gotten years ago, and part due to our short mileage each day. When I had been in South America before, I could manage 300–500 miles per day. On this trip, with our overloaded motorcycle and Donna-Rae's Parkinson's disease, we managed about 250 miles on a good day.

While Donna-Rae tried hard to be quick, we had to live with her physical disability. She could not make her hands, legs, and arms do what she used to do easily as a dancer. To close the chin strap on her helmet was as frustrating for her as trying to zip up her jacket. I sometimes found it easier for me to close her chinstrap and zip up her jacket than to stand by and watch her struggle with these simple tasks.

What would be a 10-minute "splash-and-dash" gas stop for me riding solo, easily approached 30 to 45 minutes for the two of us, sometimes an hour if she needed food to go along with the medication

Donna-Rae was as surprised as I was when the Honda slowly fell over. She could not help me lift it upright, which I did after unloading the luggage.

she needed to take. While it was frustrating for me to find myself standing in a gas station parking lot, sweating in my hot riding gear, it was more frustrating for her as she had to deal with toilets and getting into and out of her riding gear. Often rather than taking off her helmet when we stopped, she kept it on and strapped, a hot and frustrating way to get refreshed at a stop. Just before my fuse blew with her slowness, I would remind myself how lucky I was not to have to live with what she does—an unfriendly disease for which there was no cure.

What Peru did have was an abundance of small motorcycles. Most were modified into three-wheeled taxis. I often wanted to stop and take photographs of these colorful people-movers, especially the ones that were carrying goats, pigs, chickens, and once or twice a cow.

One decision I made for the Honda was to stick with the stock gas tank rather than spend $700 to $1,000 for a custom tank that would carry more fuel. We would use the savings for food, sleeping, and fuel on the trip rather than make some gas-tank-supply company a little richer.

With the stock gas tank we could usually ride 150 miles before having to switch to reserve. With careful riding at a slower speed. we could get another 20 to 30 miles on reserve. Usually there was a gas station within our 170-mile range. While the gas was plentiful, it was expensive. We often paid $5 for a gallon, and the same for a quart of oil.

Chile's desert seemed the same as before, only more dry. It was day after day of riding through some of the driest places on the planet. I was still amazed at the number of memorials that were built alongside

Not all the roads we took were paved, and often we found ourselves alone with no other vehicles or people around to help us had something gone wrong.

the road. They are put up by families to remember someone who died in an automobile or truck accident at that point of the road. Some were small, maybe only a welded car wheel with a name and dates. Others were works of art, small houses with glass windows and growing plants. For the plants to survive in the desert, someone had to water it, meaning a drive of unknown miles. Nearly every curve along the road had these memorials, and they were even on the straight sections, probably where someone fell asleep and drove off the road. Once or twice I saw multiple memorials, meaning a bus or fully loaded car took a number of lives at once.

After several days of riding across the desert, we found a small village on the ocean where we rested, enjoying the sound of waves and refreshing cool air blowing in at night. I needed to do some more writing, and it was a good time for Donna-Rae to catch up on her shopping and painting.

Argentina welcomed us with mountain scenery, blue skies, and cheap prices, and almost everything we desired, save for gas. We moved through Patagonia slowly, and then raced through our last days to cut down on the number of hours we had to spend fighting the famous Patagonia winds each day. Those winds often reached 70 miles per hour or more, which was fine when it was from behind, but ugly from the side as it tried to blow us off the road.

We rode into Ushuaia about two weeks behind schedule. This town had been our destination for nearly one year in our planning. It was an upscale town, a jumping-off place for many tourists who are booked for ship cruises to Antarctica, and so it was home to many fine restaurants, souvenir shops, and expensive hotels.

Donna-Rae had ridden as far south as I could take her on the South American continent.

We stopped and built a new stone marker where I had done the same several years before. This one lasted only one year.

We rode around town for nearly an hour trying to find an inexpensive place to stay for two or three days, but everything was about twice what we wanted to pay. About to give up and bend to the high-rent places, we were flagged down on the street by a man wearing a Norton motorcycle tee shirt who asked us if we were looking for a good-value place to stay. I cautiously answered that we were, and he told us to keep riding several blocks south and we would see his motorcycle parked out front.

"Hey, you're Jeff aren't you?" I asked. He looked at me oddly, and then said, "Yeah, how do you know me?" I laughed and said I was in his bar in Cusco, Peru, about a month earlier and had heard he was riding his Norton to Ushuaia and that there could only be one person that crazy in all of South America. He owned the Norton Rats Tavern, a motorcycle motif-filled bar, one that all traveling motorcyclists must see if they are passing through Cusco.

It was in Rio Gallegos, just two days north of Ushuaia, that I met another pair of travelers in 1997. I remember walking down the main street in town when a woman walked up to me and asked, "Are you from Montana?" It was Susan Johnson, and she and Grant had booked into the same small hotel I had for the night and seen the license plate on the back of my motorcycle. My surprise in 1997 when Susan asked me if I was from Montana was how Jeff Powers must have felt when I asked him on the street in Ushuaia if he was who I thought he was.

On February 8, Donna-Rae and I reached the end of South America, the second time by motorcycle for me, the first for her. We had a small celebration that night, then turned around and headed north to Buenos Aires from where we would fly, cruise, or swim to Africa.

We had by then ridden to Deadhorse, Alaska, and turned around and ridden to "the end of the world," the end of Route 3 on the South American continent. Our little Honda did an admirable job getting us there. Donna-Rae did an admirable job of putting up with a grouchy lone-wolf pilot.

I probably did less than an admirable job than I could have in making her ride comfortably, but I had told her I would not baby her, that I was not a caregiver. I told her she would have to toughen up on this ride around the world or throw in the towel.

I can still laugh at most of our experiences, such as the night after a hard cold riding day when I was sure the motorcycle rear shock or the frame was going to break from the hammering they were taking from our heavy load over very bad roads. We were at dinner and my body was aching. My knees hurt from having to hold the motorcycle up as Donna-Rae had gotten on and off numerous times during the day. My right wrist was throbbing at the place it was broken years ago. It was swollen from the banging it had taken through the handlebars over the bumps and potholes for the day.

I was tired, hurting, and grouchy, mostly because of all the weight we had on the motorcycle and how Donna-Rae had picked up a small rock from the road to carry as a souvenir. All I could imagine throughout the day was the expense and loss of time if the roads beat up our motorcycle enough to cause it to break.

I gulped down a beer and immediately ordered two more, confusing the waiter because he knew Donna-Rae did not drink alcohol. As the second beer was drained and the third was on its way down the same path, Donna-Rae said, "Do you think you might have a drinking problem?"

As I set the empty bottle on the table, I said, "Hell yes, I have a drinking problem. It's you." I saw her eyes swell up and start to water. I immediately knew I had made a mistake. I knew her day had been no easier than mine. I ordered a cola and said I would apologize if she did not cry, but if the tears started, I was going to order beers number four, five, and six. The tears never came, and I said, "I told you when we started on this ride, what you call your 'Riding the Dream,' that I was no bunny traveler, that going around the world with me would be hard, that I do things the hard way, like the risks, and thrive on the toughness, not the soft easy rides."

Donna-Rae smiled, called the waiter, and ordered me a beer, then said, "I just thought once in a while we could have an easy day." I realized an easy day for me was not the same for her.

The road isn't easy; death lurks on the road, behind every curve. Three of my motorcycling friends passed over while riding last year. John Richardson, known as "Little Dog," had ridden with me in Mexico, Alaska, Canada, Thailand, and elsewhere around the United States. He and I had raced motorcycles and cheated death on numerous occasions, laughing at the prospect of harm or danger. I doubt he was laughing much the day he spent an hour dying on the side of a Mexican road while riding on what I called the Curtis Circus of Death Tour.

The tour organizer wrote that I, and not he, was the cause of John's death, for not having taken John with me on my ride through South America. Another in the same group said the needless death was an "act of God." Little Dog would have doubtlessly cited other reasons in his dour way, such as foolishly following the leader. Sadly, Little Dog came back to Colorado via Fed Ex, his ashes in a plastic bag inside a small McDonald's cardboard box that had written on the side, in Spanish, "I'm loving it."

Another friend slipped on a curve with his BMW motorcycle and slid headfirst into a Porsche a few miles from his home in South Africa, just days before I was to visit him and his family. It was a sad arrival for me on the day of his funeral with his family and friends gathered at the wake, became his loss a warm and memorable evening. Shaun Powell had always gone "on the wagon" for three months each year, and the day of his funeral and evening memorial happened to coincide

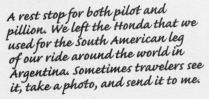

A rest stop for both pilot and pillion. We left the Honda that we used for the South American leg of our ride around the world in Argentina. Sometimes travelers see it, take a photo, and send it to me.

We crossed the Tropic of Capricorn in Africa, having done so previously in South America.

with the day he would annually fall off. It was a grand party, and the gathered friends and family celebrated as he would, had he been there.

A publisher and fellow journalist I was scheduled to work with on a coffee table book about motorcycles in 2006 lost control of a sidecar he was testing. He finished last in the survival contest with a semi-truck. I had fun with him at the Americade rally only weeks before, where we were both enjoying being part of the world's largest touring motorcycle rally. He and I viewed motorcycling in a similar manner, not as a weekender's hobby, but a 100-hour-per-week avocation and addiction.

The passing of my Harley-Davidson riding pal, "Commander Bob," may have been a blessing. He went to sleep in his favorite chair while watching TV with his wife sitting on the couch next to him. He simply did not wake up. His riding life had been tough riding. The hard stuff began when he lost a leg after hitting a bridge one night. The doctors reattached it, but he lost the other leg on a New Year's Eve when a car driver T-boned him in a parking lot while he was sitting on his bike, stationary and sober. Open heart surgery and diabetes did not keep Commander Bob off his Harley, but a crash on the way to Sturgis in 2004 slowed him up after the sidecar landed on top of him, breaking his remaining leg, ribs, and other bones.

I will eventually catch up with these friends who are riding motorcycles somewhere where they do not get cold when it rains, never having to worry about gas or flat tires, and where there are no bad roads. I miss them. I have lost four friends, but I keep their memories of our adventure.

While Donna-Rae and I were circling the globe, riding through some of the more dangerous places on the planet, I had time to reflect on how easily life can end while on a motorcycle. Screaming notices of the deaths of fellow riders and friends via e-mail made me question

Donna-Rae tries to make friends with a penguin near Cape Town, South Africa.

We used a BMW motorcycle for our tour of Africa, here reaching the farthest point south on the African continent we could ride (Cape Agulhas).

why I had been a lucky one, why I was lucky enough to still be riding. Donna-Rae and I had some close calls that could have had us returning home in a box as well (let's hope not with printing on the side saying how we were "loving it."). Numerous times we were forced off the road by oncoming vehicles. Bad road conditions or road litter and oil nearly caused us to crash in some ugly countries where medical facilities were at the lowest levels on the earth. Donna-Rae said she was my (our) lucky penny. I countered with that we were lucky because the heavy medication she was taking chilled her out, keeping her from jerking when road conditions made the motorcycle want to do things I had to fight to keep us upright. She never so much as twitched in these situations, when the slightest twitch might have caused us to crash.

Riding around the world with a female passenger who liked to stop to photograph castles, souvenir shops, and stone ruins, things I usually rode past, was new for me. While I was trying to adapt to two-up global touring from my lone-wolf style, the death of friends haunted me. Compounding the stress from those factors was a tight timeline and light wallet.

Safari by motorcycle was the plan for Africa. We had planned to ride through inexpensive Africa on a true motorcycle safari. We were going to purchase or rent a large motorcycle, then lease a fully outfitted

Land Rover for desert and jungle travel to follow them. The Land Rover would solve one of the biggest problems Donna-Rae had faced on her adventure: where to carry all the souvenirs she was purchasing. There was little room to carry items such as inexpensive handmade capes, caps, and gloves on the already overburdened motorcycle. She had to resort to mailing parcels home at a cost that made the items no longer the "deals" she thought they were. Having an empty Land Rover following them meant that weight and space would no longer be a point of contention between the pilot (Greg) and the pillion (Donna-Rae) as we plowed through deep sands of deserts such as the Kalahari or the jungle mud and swamps of the Okavango River along the Namibian and Angola border. Not only could the Land Rover carry Donna-Rae's purchases, but also the tent, sleeping bags, and luggage, making my daily manhandling of the overburdened motorcycle much easier.

Of course, we needed someone to drive the Land Rover. I recommended we hire a local native, someone who knew the deserts and jungles but who would also be appreciative of the opportunity for work, three solid meals each day, and driving a 4x4 all-terrain vehicle. We conjured a modern-day bearer who would drive the Land Rover behind the motorcycle. Ideally, at the end of the riding day, the bearer (I dubbed him "Moses") would do the donkey work of unloading the luggage, erecting the tent, laying out the sleeping bags, constructing a latrine, then preparing dinner, which Moses would serve on a cloth-covered table underneath an awning. As Donna-Rae and I watched the sunset, Moses would wash the dishes, scrounge firewood, and quietly play a drum to coax wildlife away from the campsite. Throughout the

While we were all smiles for the camera, the stress of being together was starting to wear us down.

I had covered much of Africa before, so I chose some new roads, this one being gravel. Donna-Rae told me later she thought it was the main road.

night, Moses would tend the fire and ward off unwelcome visitors. In the morning, as Donna-Rae and I would eat Moses' prepared breakfast, he would break camp, then lug and pack all the luggage in the Land Rover. I would not be wearing myself out in the 100-degree heat before starting a long day of hard riding and could be concerned only with the maintenance and piloting of the motorcycle. But that was all a dream.

Donna-Rae wanted to shop and see animals and trees in Africa. I was more interested is trying to avoid being run over by an elephant in Botswana or a minivan taxi in Cape Town or Johannesburg. Trying to make those two agendas mesh took away the job for Moses. What Donna-Rae did not know was nearly all the wild game in Africa had been killed for food. The animals left survived in private game reserves or national parks. A famed park, such as Etosha in northern Namibia, prohibited motorcycles, thus requiring an expensive car or guided tour. The same with the Kruger National Park in South Africa. Most of the private game reserves carried visitors through on viewing vehicles, often another expensive guided tour.

The prices for rental motorcycles were reasonable if we wanted to rent something in the small scooter range, but for what we needed we were looking at $250 per day plus $1,000 deposit, which was rumored to be seldom returned. If we were going to circle around in Africa for two months, waiting for warm weather for the next leg of our ride to the North Cape in Norway, a rental motorcycle was going to cost us as much as purchasing a new $20,000 model. To purchase a used motorcycle was also going to be expensive due to the high import taxes.

We also discovered the price of a leased Land Rover was in the Bill Gates budget, not the Donna-Rae and Greg budget. For even a small car it was going to cost at least $100 per day, and it was prohibited from leaving South Africa. When vehicle rental, safari fees, food, gas, visas, and sleeping arrangements were totaled, the figure staggered Donna-Rae. "If we go that way, there won't be any money left for shopping," she said.

As we worked on our options, it became clear there was going to be no room in the budget for the Land Rover, and if there was no Land Rover there would be no need for Moses, leaving the idea of a Moses dead. For some wiggle room for miscellaneous items (curios and souvenirs), we purchased two $18 sleeping bags before we left Cape Town. We were off to look at curios, souvenirs, trees, and animals for Donna-Rae, with the possibility of meeting other international motorcycle travelers for me to trade travel stories with and take photographs for a new book I was working on.

One of Donna-Rae's continuing adventures was that of ablutions, day and night. I was helpful with tips such as, "Always carry a stash of toilet paper in a pocket," and "Look down and around before you squat, whether indoors or out." Donna-Rae's biggest challenge in this adventure category was taking care of her business after dark. She woke me with her concerns that anything from a leopard to a crocodile was lurking just outside or rubbing up against the tent. I sometimes slapped the side of the tent to make noise to scare away the animal, or I handed her the flashlight and told her to look outside the tent entrance flap and see for herself that what she was hearing was the wind or branches rustling against the tent. With her contact lenses out, she felt sure she would see no animals, take care of her needs, then quickly return, leaving me to my rest.

One night when I needed to make a midnight water pass, I took the flashlight to make sure I did not step on any snakes. As I was watering the jungle bushes, I aimed the light around the perimeter of our tent and saw several pairs of glowing yellow eyes staring back. They were either hyenas or large cats. As I zipped-up I thought, "Hmmmm, Donna-Rae came here to see animals. I wonder what she will think about those when she has to make her outdoor visit tonight?" As I slipped back into my sleeping bag, Donna-Rae anxiously asked if I had

I had tried riding an ostrich on a previous trip to Africa and convinced Donna-Rae it was not that hard. She was hesitant to climb on because each time she tried, the ostrich turned its head and snarled at her.

seen anything. I answered, "Not a single snake or bird," then went blissfully to sleep.

One of the problems associated with travel on a motorcycle is that there are often places motorcycles are either prohibited or where physically it is impossible to ride them. One of those places was the huge sand dunes of the Sossusvlei National Park in Namibia. Here it would have been impossible to ride a heavily loaded touring motorcycle because the wheels would immediately sink into the soft sand. Instead, Donna-Rae and I climbed on a four-wheel-drive truck that ferried us to the famed dunes to film a sunrise. As the sun came up, the color of the dunes changed from dark brown to red, then white, all within a matter of minutes.

To get around the world by motorcycle means having to use more than a motorcycle. To cross oceans, seas, lakes and rivers, the motorcycle has to be flown or floated, and also negotiated through unfriendly countries that do not issue transit visas for American citizens. Then there were the large expanses of swamps or impassable mountain passes. Other times, for security or safety reasons, it was better to try to blend in with the locals and not stand out by riding an expensive motorcycle costing 1,000 times more than the average local worker earns in a year. This may mean hiding the motorcycle in a truck, then using the local means of transportation.

Some of the places Donna-Rae and I traveled were well away from paved roads. We often saw animals that disappeared before we could capture them in the camera. The best time for animal viewing was at dusk as the four-legged hunters would start their evening prowling and growling. Bunny-hugger that I am, I often waited long after the campfire had died down to hear the primal screams of the hunted being caught by the hunters. Donna-Rae would likewise wait for the sounds of the hunters, more anxiously than me, often believing they were sniffing or padding within inches of her inside the tent.

The government of Namibia had refused to place the cheetah on the endangered species list although there were few left in the wild. As meat eaters, cheetahs were often the targets of farmers who feared the loss of their goats and sheep, so shooting them had greatly reduced their numbers. One farmer had set aside a large portion of his farm as a safe haven for cheetahs. He struggled to find the 6 pounds of fresh meat each of his 20 to 30 cheetahs needed to survive daily. The Namibian government allowed him to keep the cheetahs but did not allow him to breed them nor did they offer any assistance. The males were kept in a 20- to 30-acre open compound and the females in another. Donna-Rae bought enough fresh meat for one cheetah each, and then rode in the back of a pick-up truck through the compounds

In Italy, we wanted to see how far the Leaning Tower of Pisa was leaning.

while the cheetahs followed what they knew was their daily meat wagon. The intensity of the yellow-and-black cat eyes left no doubt about what would happen if a hand did not release the meat soon enough as it was tossed outward. These were wild cheetahs, not the docile ones found in a zoo. The snarling and fighting that took place when a flank of meat hit the ground showed why the big cats were no house pets.

Safety was a constant concern as we traveled through Africa. There were numerous warnings about wandering away from the campfire at night where two- or four-legged hunters lurked, some looking for money and valuables, others looking for a meal of meat on two legs.

Donna-Rae had great difficulty making her camera work with the advancing Parkinson's affecting her hands. Sometimes a stop to take one picture took 15–30 minutes.

We camped when possible to save costs as we moved north through Europe. These were tough nights because Donna-Rae was losing some of her mobility and could not help much with setting up or taking down our tent, but she never complained.

During daylight hours, danger arrived in the form of broken sections of road, errant drivers, and domestic animals such as sheep, dogs, and goats crossing in front of drivers.

Once an oncoming truck swerved into our lane to avoid hitting deep potholes in the truck's lane, believing I would steer the motorcycle off the road and into the ditch rather than take the truck head-on. At 70 miles per hour, I frantically tried to slow the motorcycle while weighing my options. I immediately ruled out the head-on alternative as the truck driver had guessed I would. Quickly glancing at the ditch, I sensed death written for Donna-Rae and me on the rocks, if not from the crash, then from the hundreds of miles that lay between us and the nearest hospital. I picked option three. I switched lanes, taking the chance that we'd miss the bombed-out broken macadam in the opposite lane.

Later in the day I said I should not have given the one-fingered salute to the truck that tried to run us off the road. "What truck?" Donna-Rae asked. "When did that happen?" I explained the situation and our luck, leaving Donna-Rae worried about the next truck. One of the side effects from the medication Donna-Rae took for her Parkinson's Disease was she often fell asleep on the back of the motorcycle while leaning up against my back. While I was dodging the oncoming truck and refrigerator-sized potholes, Donna-Rae had been soundly sleeping. I shook my head and said, "I really ought to start taking the pills you're taking, especially when I cannot sleep at night from the stress of riding all day."

As we wandered around some of the more remote areas in southern Africa, we were able to find nearly everything we needed from gasoline to laundry facilities. In Zimbabwe, gasoline was scarce but available if we were willing to buy it out of 1-liter Pepsi bottles or hand-pumped from a 50-gallon drum behind a shack in a village. A stop for the night at a tourist lodge on the Okavango River, looking across at Angola where people and drums were heard throughout the night, found a computer on a handmade table in a shed connected to the Internet. It was available for use for $10 per hour.

Another evening found a well-stocked, rough-hewn bar on the banks of the Okavango River, where we drank some beer and listened to a cassette tape play the Doors as crocodiles and hippopotamuses lay 50 feet away. The swimming pool in that campground was a wire mesh cage suspended from floating 50-gallon drums in the river, much like a shark cage. The toilet was called the "loo with a view," because it was an open porcelain throne set high enough in the bush for the sitter to enjoy a good view of the swamp and animals surrounding it.

In Botswana, elephants were kept out of the campground (and from walking over tents) by electrified fences. The biggest threat while camping in Botswana (besides the snakes) were the monkeys and baboons. Both found easy pickings of everything from purses to food from tourists not securing everything in their tents or cars. One evening a monkey was bold enough to rush into the cooking area and snatch an unopened bag of cookies Donna-Rae was reserving for dessert.

For Donna-Rae, Africa was a learning experience. For me, who had traveled there four times before, it was a reinforcement of much of what I had learned before. Some of our Southern Africa teachings include the following:

1. Never assume anything; life was different from what we were used to in the United States.
2. If a sign says "Open 24 hours," that does not mean 24 in a row.

3. To plan on how long something will take to accomplish, add three hours, then double it.
4. What is on a menu does not mean what is available.
5. While chewing on food and something unexpectedly crunches, swallow and accept it.
6. While toilet paper is not scarce in stores, it is always scarce when camping and in most public facilities.
7. A bathroom is a room where you take a bath. A toilet is what you are asking for when you ask where a bathroom is.
8. When someone tells you they will be with you "Just now," it does not mean, "I will be with you shortly." It means, "I will be with you when, and if, I feel like it, or maybe never."
9. When tourist agents say they will call you back or e-mail you, they mean "Just now."
10. National holidays are chosen randomly.
11. Americans are not always welcome.
12. Red lights and stop signs sometimes mean stop, but often just mean "slow down" or even "speed up."
13. Painted lines on road surfaces are for decoration not traffic control.
14. A fool and his or her money are quickly parted whether by theft or sales.
15. Never leave anything you cannot live without out of your sight or unattended, such as a motorcycle helmet or gloves hanging on the handlebars or a packsack under your chair while eating.
16. Passports, cash, credit cards, and traveler's checks should be kept close at hand, hidden and secure. A tourist without a passport is a tourist without a country and one without money is in the worst kind of trouble.

We were blessed with good weather as we rode north through Sweden.

17. Do not expect to find things being done as they are in the United States. One of the reasons for travel away from home is to find different things.

18. When buying souvenirs or curios, plan on a half-day to get them packaged and then into the local postal system to send home, then add most of the rest of the day as a lost travel day due to the time spent finding tape, transporting boxes to the post office, and finding a cash machine or bank to pay for the postage.

Ferryboats are everywhere to be found from the north of Africa to the south of Europe. Some were little more than a cargo ferry carrying trucks across the Mediterranean Sea. Others were overnight luxury liners with restaurants, bars, and duty-free shopping stores. Sleeping on the overnighters was optional: a berth in a shared room or deck chairs. Because Donna-Rae and I were ahead of the tourist season, and on a motorcycle, we were able to enjoy a comfortable night crossing in a room with a shower and toilet that would cost nearly twice as much a few weeks later. Donna-Rae, a sunset-sunrise photographer, caught both with her camera. I relished not having to shovel coal deep in the heated bowels of a freighter, and snoozed in clean sheets, reading a book from time to time.

In Norway, we stopped to purchase some postcards, about the only souvenirs we had room for on the motorcycle.

Sicily was a first time visit for both of us. Donna-Rae wanted to spend time riding along the coast, listening to the waves crashing at night. I wanted to hunt small twisty mountain roads I had noted on the map as well as see the home of the Mafia depicted in so many novels and films. We both agreed the explosive Mount Etna deserved our attention.

We were thankfully a few weeks ahead of the tourist season, when prices for pensions, guesthouses, and hotels would double. We managed to find a clean and inexpensive tourist apartment near the beach that fit our meager budget. With a kitchen, cable TV, and private veranda where the motorcycle could be parked, we cooked meals, caught up on writing, transferred photos to CDs, and watched the news of the world. Donna-Rae played tourist by haggling with souvenir vendors enough to fill another box to be mailed home for her daughters and grandchildren. I watched CNN and the BBC while performing routine maintenance to the motorcycle on the veranda.

After a visit to the post office to jettison Donna-Rae's souvenirs, we rode to Palermo. Here we found 90-degree temps, traffic-choked streets, and polluted air. An hour of sitting on top of a hot motorcycle (the gasoline in the gas tank was boiling!) and inhaling exhaust fumes from trucks, cars, and thousands of motor scooters was enough to convince me that finding the Mafia dens was not worth sucking in the stink of the street. "This part of the toe of the boot of Italy smells of cheese feet, worse than some backpacker's we've met in youth hostels," I said. Donna-Rae self-injected more eye drops, coughed up some yellow goop, and then said, "Can we leave?" I pointed the

Some nights we opted for camper cabins rather than set up our tent. About every third or fourth night we would spend the big money and take a hotel or guesthouse room for warmth and a shower.

66° 32' 35'

Crossing the Arctic Circle, which we had done before in Alaska.

motorcycle south and we fled to the clean air and twisty roads of the high mountains in the center of the island.

Back on the mainland of Italy, the next stop was Pompeii. To get there, we rode some of the famed Autostrade of Italy, where we were passed at 100 miles per hour by cars clocking near 150 miles per hour. The high-speed roads were a fast way to move around Italy, but came at a price, as most were toll roads. An additional cost was the lower miles per gallon needed to maintain the 90 to 100 miles per hour while riding in the middle lane of the three lanes moving in their direction. The far right lane was for the much slower vehicles, such as trucks and slow cars. The left lane was for the big dogs, BMWs and Mercedes that flew at speeds close to airplane lift-off levels. One crash resulted in a 15-mile traffic stall while police and maintenance people cleaned up the scene. Fortunately for us, as well as other motorcyclists, we were allowed to ride between the stopped cars, "splitting lanes." What could have been a several-hour delay turned out to be little more than a slowdown. Motorcycles were often seen riding between cars, even when the cars and trucks were moving, sometimes at speeds near 60 miles per hour. I opted to go with the flow at speeds above 40 miles per hour, but when things slowed down I joined the locals and took advantage of the opportunity offered to motorcycles.

More camping to manage our dwindling budget.

A rest stop found us fighting mosquitoes as thick as we had found in Alaska.

"People, people, people" was how I described much of Italy. I noted that nearly anywhere houses could be constructed, they had been. In the cities, the streets were jammed with traffic, and villages and towns filled the countryside. My "people, people, people" comment was usually followed by, "The Italians are following too literally the Pope's condemnation of condoms. They need to pull up on their baby making or soon there will be no clean air or space on mountain sides to build houses the way they are following the gospel. The rhythm method or their timing isn't working."

Eventually we tired of fighting city traffic to find a place to sleep at night and started looking in the countryside for small guesthouses, which cost less than hotels and were often owner-operated, with family members doing the cooking and cleaning. English was seldom spoken in the smaller villages where we spent the night, so Donna-Rae found herself trying to recall the Italian she had learned nearly 40 years earlier. When she spoke Italian, it sometimes came out as a mix of Italian and leftover Spanish from months earlier when we passed through South America.

One night Donna-Rae ordered broccoli and was served what she thought was spinach. She complained to the waiter by saying, in her mixed Italian/Spanish/English, "I ordered broccoli and this is spinach." The waiter answered, in English, "That is broccoli madam." She repeated her complaint, and the waiter repeated his answer. Finally I said to Donna-Rae, "Eat your broccoli, Donna-Rae." Donna-Rae snapped back, "But it's not broccoli, it's spinach." I swirled the wine in my glass, took a sip, then gazed at the ceiling, saying, "Remember what is said about doing Roman things when in Rome? We are 50 miles from Rome. That spinach on your plate is broccoli. You ordered broccoli, broccoli is what you were brought, so you should be enjoying it." Donna-Rae scowled at both the waiter and me, then politely said,

"I don't like spinach." Both the waiter and I lifted our eyebrows while looking at each other, as if to say, "Momma mia!" The broccoli went untouched during the rest of the meal.

Donna-Rae wanted to see Pisa and the leaning tower. She also itched to shop at the tourist market in Florence. Both were added to the route plan. While she shopped for two hours in Florence, I made friends with a street artist doing oil paintings in the public square to sell to tourists. The Florentine artist, wearing a tilted beret over his flowing white hair, turned out to be a relocated hippie from California who had learned Italian from a girlfriend and how to smear paint in the sixties. He said he usually sold $200 to $400 worth of his self-described "junk" to tourists each day, usually Americans. I asked him if he thought there might be room for one more Native painter on the square, meaning myself. The artist answered, "Nah, most of us here have the best places staked out. Someone would have to die first, and at what we can make in a good week off the tourists, that's not gonna happen real quick. A dead woman's son filled the last spot that was open."

The ride through Switzerland was short. Most of the high passes were still closed due to the snow, not slated to open until mid- or late June. At $20 for a plate of spaghetti with tomato sauce, and $4 for a small Coke, Donna-Rae and I left Switzerland to the ultra-rich residents such as Tina Turner. We settled for food in a supermarket just over the border in Austria where many of the nearby Swiss residents shopped. There, lunch was only $10 and a Coke $2.

The plan for this leg of the trip was to ride to the North Cape of Norway, the northernmost point on the European continent we could ride. Unfortunately the weather in Europe had not liked our plan. Germany and points north were suffering from cold and rain, even though it was late spring. We motorcycled around Germany, waiting for the weather to warm up in the north, which it never did. During our wandering, we managed to attend a motorcycle travelers meeting, sponsored by the Touratech company, a firm specializing in parts and modifications for motorcycles used by long-distance travelers. I knew several of the other journalists attending the meeting as well as a number of the attendees. I had given a presentation four years earlier at a BMW motorcycle meeting near Munich and many of the people attending the Touratech meeting remembered me from that earlier meeting. Nearly 3,000 attended the Touratech gathering and Donna-Rae made new friends through my numerous contacts. She was fascinated with the enthusiasm and support the motorcycle travelers exhibited at our kind of travel.

The motorcycle we used for the North Cape leg of our 'round-the-world ride was a BMW K100 RT, probably the only one in Europe with

Donna-Rae had reached another end of the earth, as far north as we could go on the European continent.

aluminum panniers attached. The plush seat, wind protection, and smooth engine made it ideal for riding the pavement of Europe. There was little off-road or gravel riding on the route to the North Cape, as most of the roads were paved. I tried to avoid any off-pavement riding, knowing that the big touring motorcycle "likes to lay down on its side when off pavement."

The motorcycle was designed for high-speed autobahn travel, and that was much of what we did from the toe of the boot of Italy to the middle of Germany. At $30 for a tank of gas, with three fill-ups each day, the BMW was expensive to run, but it was an expense we couldn't get away from.

We reached the North Cape in Norway on a cold and windy day.

We were still friends when we returned to Germany.

Where we could save money was on eating and sleeping. Donna-Rae learned that while she and I disliked American fast food from McDonald's, we could get good value for our money when stopping at the Golden Arches. Neither of us ordered the burgers. Instead we chose the salads, fries, and mineral water, often half of what we would pay for the same in a restaurant. Sleeping indoors consumed more of our travel funds than expected, because cold weather and closed campgrounds (too early for the tourist season) forced us indoors. European friends would laugh when we complained about the high prices, saying, "If you think this is expensive, wait until you get to Norway." Both Donna-Rae and I decided the run to the North Cape

might be a time to lose some of the excess body baggage we acquired in Argentina and from pasta and wine (me) in Italy. We sprayed waterproofing material on our cheap tent, motorcycle jackets, boots, and gloves, and then headed north.

We made the ride to the North Cape a quick one due to the cold and the expense of travel up and back to Germany. When we returned to Germany, we had several options for crossing Asia; the most expensive and slowest was to simply ride a train and ship the motorcycle across. Iran, Bhutan, and Myanmar were all going to be "no-go" areas that we would have to fly the motorcycle over, an expense we decided was foolish. Instead, we put the BMW back in storage and used our money to fly to Nepal where we had planned on buying a used motorcycle to try to enter India. Another factor that played into our decision to fly over Greece, Turkey, Iran, and Pakistan was we were running out of time, and each of us wanted to return home to our projects there.

Going Down to Kat-Kat-Kat-Kathmandu

Spit on. That is what happened to Donna-Rae as she was leaving one of the temples in Kathmandu, Nepal. A woman spat a wad of phlegm on her. It was a new experience for her, an old one for me. When we talked about the incident later that evening, I said it proved that traveling shows how wrong one can be about a country.

The spitter did not know if Donna-Rae was from Austria or Alaska, only that she saw a white Western face. I put a positive side to it by saying, "So she spit on your back, no big deal. The last time I got spit on by a woman it was from the front, but all she could manage splatting was my boot. Of course that was by a bitch-born daughter of Hades who was hot because I would not pay for her favors. I forgot about that until you reminded me. What I haven't forgotten are the camels that spit on me. Now camels, they can really let a honker fly with deadly aim. And like the woman who spit on you, she has no clue; you're just a target."

Motorcycles had multiplied since I was in Kathmandu several years ago; there were motorcycle rental businesses everywhere. Part of it was from the influx of inexpensive motorcycles on the streets, small displacement motorcycles from China. Another part was from the

While Donna-Rae shopped in Hong Kong, I was thankful I did not have to deal with traffic in this bustling city.

219

A final meal in Asia and then we were headed back to the United States, 14 months after we had started. It had been a long, strange trip around the world.

rising capital of entrepreneurs in Kathmandu, the major city in Nepal. Tourists had the money to rent motorcycles, creating a demand; naturally a group rose to meet it. A small rental bike, big enough to haul Donna-Rae and me around, cost about $10 per day (not a bad deal compared to the $250 a day rental agencies charged for bigger bikes in California or Germany).

In Nepal, we had to decide between riding a motorcycle across the country or circling around it, then arrange to fly over Bhutan, India, Burma, and into Thailand. I wanted to take a rental motorcycle and hunt a Yeti in the Annapurna Conservation Area. Donna-Rae wanted to taste, buy, touch, and smell all that differed from West to East. It was a hard time for both. In the end, the Maoists, police, overbearing sickness, and maybe even Buddha made the decisions for us.

While I hunted the streets of Kathmandu for a large motorcycle, Donna-Rae looked in at shops, stupas, temples, burning corpses, and Freak Street. She was enjoying the various tourist opportunities, especially the inexpensive shopping.

Donna-Rae's Parkinson's medicine, while questionable about dealing with Parkinson's disease, seemed to make her body impregnable against other germs, viruses, or bugs. Not so for my daily vitamins. A serious intestinal amoebic bug grabbed me in Kathmandu and halted my hunt for Yeti. While Donna-Rae shopped, I was dropped. I forgot about motorcycles, riding good roads, and hunting Yetis. What I thought about was toilets, toilet paper, then Vaseline, and how Buddha may have not wanted me to hunt Yeti. As I wandered the streets of Kathmandu, moving from one toilet to the next, I forgot about trying to manage the freakish paperwork and expense of trying to ride through Bhutan, India, Burma, and then into Thailand.

Freak Street in Kathmandu was the end of the Hippie Highway, famous in the late sixties for hashish bars, cheap lodging, and trading tales of what had happened to the travelers from Marrakech, Morocco, the beginning of the road. Donna-Rae wanted to see what it was like today, but street demonstrations halted her walking expedition. It was riot time in Kathmandu, and the anti-government parades were being met by government officials swinging batons, shooting guns, and tossing tear-gas canisters. Any leftover hippie from the sixties would have had enough sense to blow town and not weed, which is what Donna-Rae and I decided to do, as we didn't smoke but were on enough prescribed drugs to keep a gorilla zonked.

We flew to Thailand, where I had another motorcycle in storage. From there we had hoped to cross Laos or Cambodia and enter Vietnam if weather conditions allowed. I had ridden some of the roads before and knew they were unpaved in areas, but entering Vietnam was going to be the biggest problem. Only big-money travelers were riding into Vietnam, some paying thousands just to say they rode their motorcycle there. We found ourselves again weighing the costs of traveling farther on my motorcycle as well as having to deal with the time we would lose. The clock to return home was ticking louder.

Another problem Donna-Rae was experiencing was her drugs for Parkinson's seemed to be working less each day, and she could not find replacements in the countries we had been passing through. Several attempts to try locally prescribed alternatives had caused serious loss of memory and hallucinations. We had two incidents where she would go out alone from our hotel and become disoriented and become lost, once in the lobby of the hotel. We had to make a tough decision based on my inability to be with her 24 hours each day and how well she could do sitting on the back of the motorcycle while hallucinating. She was also losing some of her physical abilities to the point of nearly not being able to climb on to the back of a motorcycle, even a small one. It was an ugly time, but we agreed she needed to get back to her own physicians who had been administering her medications while the Parkinson's was changing her mental abilities.

Thailand was wet. Rain had caused the Ping River to rise above its banks. It was the worst flooding in 40 years. Motorcycle gear that I had stored high and dry when I left two years earlier was covered in mud and growing green fungus. Friends' motorcycles in the same room had water over the seats. It was a dirty time. A check on the conditions of the roads to Ankor Wat in Cambodia and the Plain of Jars on Laos resulted in messages such as, "Forget it. Come back in three or four months. It's still raining here. The only way to visit now is by airplane."

We circled around in wet Thailand while information flowed in with the rain. We decided not to tax our hammered budget with further flights, hotels, and rental of four-wheel-drive vehicles. We parked our motorcycle on high ground, shipped some packages home, and flew onto our next stop, Hong Kong, and from there back to the United States, where we collected another of my stored motorcycles.

Now began the long ride home to Colorado for Donna-Rae and Montana, for me. As fall began, we could start to slide back into our former lives as mother-grandmother and writer-fisherman. We had thousands of photographs to review, sort, and file. Souvenirs had to be unboxed and gifts had to be sent. I had to face the reality of some serious slippage in writing deadlines. Donna-Rae had to finish her book. It was a busy fall ahead for both of us. As we looked over our shoulders at the nearly 50,000 kilometers of roads we had covered, it had been, as I wrote in my logbook so long ago, "a long, strange ride" around the world.

Index